Raniero Cantalamessa

The Mystery of God's Word

Translated by
Alan Neame

A Liturgical Press Book

THE LITURGICAL PRESS
Collegeville, Minnesota

Cover design by Ann Blattner.
Icon: The Savior in Power (15th century), Tretjakov Gallery, Moscow.

First published in Italian under the title *"Ci ha parlato nel Figlio." Il mistero della parola di Dio* by Editrice Àncora in Milan.

Published in the United States of America.

5	6	7	8

Library of Congress Cataloging-in-Publication Data

Cantalamessa, Raniero.
   ["Ci ha parlato nel Figlio." Il mistero della parola di Dio. English]
   The mystery of God's word / Raniero Cantalamessa ; Alan
Neame, translator.
     p.   cm.
   ISBN 0-8146-2127-9
   1. Jesus Christ—Preaching. 2. Bible. N.T.—Criticism,
interpretation, etc. 3. Catholic Church—Liturgy—Theology.
I. Title.
BT590.P7C36 1994
232.9'54—dc20   93-40552
                                           CIP

Contents

Chapter I

"JESUS BEGAN TO PREACH"

The mystery of the Word of God in salvation-history

After describing the baptism of Jesus, the evangelist Mark continues his narrative by saying that "Jesus came to Galilee proclaiming the gospel of God: 'This is the time of fulfillment. The kingdom of God is at hand. Repent and believe in the Gospel' " (Mark 1:14f.). Matthew writes more briefly: "From that time on, Jesus began to preach and say, 'Repent, for the kingdom of heaven is at hand' " (Matt 4:17).

These are the opening words of the gospel, meaning the good news "of" Jesus (that is to say, brought by Jesus) and not merely the good news "about" Jesus. The evangelists say, "Jesus began to preach and say, 'Repent . . .' " They thus emphasize two quite distinct things: first, the fact that he preached; and second, what he preached, the principal matter being repentance. What will concern us is not so much the things about which God speaks to us, as the fact, disturbing in itself, that God does speak to us: God's speaking. Since, however, God speaks about his Word in the Bible, that is to say he expresses himself (and how powerfully he does so!) about his speech with us human beings, our meditation will not be on an abstract and purely formal theme but, quite the reverse, on a real and absolutely concrete one that occupies the very heart of Scripture. "The Lord has spoken," says the Bible (Ps 50:1) in tacit and continuous polemic against those gods of the nations who "have mouths but speak not" (Ps 115:5). In these meditations let us try our best to listen, in fear and trembling, to this speaking God; let us try our best to accept his heartbroken invitation: "Listen, my people, I want to speak" (cf. Ps 50:7).

It is my intention to let the Word speak, rather than speak myself about the Word; to make sure the Word never becomes a mere object, but ever remains the subject speaking to us with divine authority, before whom we can but exclaim with the infant

5

Samuel: "Speak, Lord, for your servant is listening!" (1 Sam 3:9). Nothing is more sure than this, that God speaks; yet we feel the need to pray to him, "Speak, Lord!" since it is one thing that he should speak but quite another that he should speak to us so that we can hear his voice. And so, let us beseech him truly, from the heart, now: Lord, do not allow us to run through the pages of your Bible without, somewhere, encountering you as you still "move about" in the paradise of your Scriptures; we creatures of nothing, may we dare to venture out on the open sea of your Wisdom; send your divine breath, the Holy Spirit, so that we may indeed commit ourselves to the deep and come to you across the waters. Give us a simple heart, able to marvel and leap at the sound of your voice, as children leap to the voice of their father, as friends to that of their friend, and the bride to that of the bridegroom. With the bride in the Song of Songs, we beseech you: "Let us hear your voice!"

1. *Preaching in the life of Jesus*

The gospel words quoted above describe an event occupying a very precise position in time and space: it occurs in fact "in Galilee," "after John had been arrested." The event itself is contained in these words: "Jesus began to preach." The words used in this context by the evangelists forcefully stress that here we are dealing with a beginning, something new not only in the life of Jesus but in salvation-history itself. It is the start of a special time, a new *kairos,* of salvation, lasting for some two and a half years (from the autumn of A.D. 27 to the spring of A.D. 30), until the time of Jesus' death. It is the time of the preaching of the kingdom. The importance Jesus attached to this activity of his was such that he could say he had been sent from the Father and consecrated with the unction of the Spirit especially for this purpose, that is, "to bring glad tidings to the poor" (Luke 4:18). On one occasion when people wanted to detain him, he urged the apostles to leave, saying to them, "Let us go on to the nearby villages so that I can preach there too; for this is the purpose for which I have come" (cf. Mark 1:38).

So far I have spoken of the time when the preaching took place; but it is not a matter merely of a time, but also of a mystery;

6

and it is as such that we now approach it. By the word *mystery* we mean an event in the life of Jesus that conveys a salvific meaning and is celebrated as such by the Church in the liturgy. Now, it is true there is no specific liturgical feast of Jesus' preaching (as there is for his birth, his transfiguration, his death, and so forth), but it is also true that throughout the liturgy the Church recalls Christ's preaching. The Liturgy of the Word, which is an integral part of every Mass, is nothing other than the liturgical actualization of the preaching Christ. A Vatican II text reads: "Christ is present in his word, since it is he himself who speaks when the Holy Scriptures are read in the church."[1] As, *in history,* having preached the kingdom of God, Jesus goes up to Jerusalem to offer himself in sacrifice to the Father, so, *in the liturgy,* having once again proclaimed his word, Jesus renews his self-offering to the Father through the Eucharistic action. When, at the end of the Preface, we say, "Blessed is he who comes in the name of the Lord; hosanna in the highest," we are in fact referring to that moment when Jesus enters Jerusalem to celebrate his Passover there: when the time of preaching is over and the time of the passion begins.

It has been said that the gospels came into being as "passion-narratives with extended introductions." This means just one thing: that the apostles regarded the account of what Jesus said as an indispensable introduction for an understanding of what he did, that is to say his passion and death. The Church, in consequence, by prefixing a Liturgy of the Word to the Eucharistic liturgy properly so-called, has thus done no more than maintain this sequence, linking preaching to passion, Word to Eucharist.

Jesus' preaching is thus a mystery since it not only contains the revelation of a doctrine but explains the very mystery of Christ's person; it is essential for an understanding of both what goes before (the mystery of the incarnation) and what comes after (the paschal mystery). Without the words of Jesus, these events would be mute.

2. The Word of Christ and the Word of the prophets

The opening words of the Epistle to the Hebrews help us to widen our horizon and contemplate Jesus' preaching, no longer only in the context of his earthly life, but also in that of the entire sweep of salvation-history: "In times past, God spoke in partial and various ways to our ancestors through the prophets; in these last days, he spoke to us through the Son" (cf. Heb 1:1-2). In what does the difference between the word of the prophets and that of the Son consist? The prophets introduced their words with the formula "Thus says Yahweh," or "Oracle of the Lord!" Jesus begins with "I say to you." Moreover, sometimes he reinforces this "I" by prefixing "Amen" to it: "Amen, I say to you . . ." (Mark 3:28), something for which there is no parallel in the whole of Jewish literature. "In the *Amen* preceding 'I say to you' all Christology is contained in essence" (H. Schlier); with this formula Jesus expresses his absolute certainty that he is speaking in God's name, with the authority of God himself.

Jesus gives the impression of speaking on his own account, not of just commenting on previous spiritual masters like all the other rabbis of his day. Indeed, he puts himself above even the Bible, not hesitating on occasion to modify and improve it; his Sermon on the Mount is based entirely on the scheme "You have heard that it was said . . . but I say to you" (cf. Matt 5:21f.). The impression inevitably caused by such a way of speaking was enormous. It was more or less as though one fine day one of us priests, addressing the folk in church, should start altering the gospel and saying: "Jesus Christ told you . . . but I tell you . . ." So the reaction of his listeners is easy to understand: "The people were astonished at his teaching, for he taught them as one having authority, and not as the scribes" (Mark 1:22). The term most commonly used to express the impression of novelty made by Jesus' words is precisely this "authority" (cf. also Mark 11:28). The soldier sent to arrest him put the same thing more simply: "No one has ever spoken like this man" (cf. John 7:46).

Along with this sovereign authority and absolute independence, we also note in Jesus an absolute dependence. He says, "My teaching is not my own but is from the one who sent me" (John 7:16); "The word you hear is not mine but that of the Father who sent me" (John 14:24). Jesus says, "My word is not mine," and yet, St. Augustine observes, he himself is "the Word"; it is as though he were saying, "I am not mine, I do not belong to myself!"[2]

Hence the secret of Jesus' authority is his obedience and total submission to the Father. He states that his words are not his own, but the Father's, and this places him in the ranks of the prophets; but then he adds, "The Father and I are one" (John 10:30), and this places him infinitely above all the prophets! Jesus is "the radiance of the glory and the imprint of the substance" of the Father (cf. Heb 1:3); later the Church was to say that he is consubstantial with the Father. So the difference lies in the fact that, first, in the Old Testament, God spoke to us through intermediary persons, but now he speaks to us in person, since the Son is himself "God from God."

What is new concerns not only the *way* God speaks (through the Son, and not through the prophets) but also the *content;* and this concerns God himself. The *Abbà* uttered by his Son during the days he lived on earth unveiled depths of God hitherto unknown, revealed the Trinity! Jesus says, "No one knows the Father except the Son" (Matt 11:27): we for our part understand these words as meaning that no one could know *who* the Father was before Jesus. However, their meaning is much more radical: no one could know that *there was* a Father, that God is a Father (and a real Father of a real Son) before Jesus revealed this! Indeed, as St. Irenaeus said, Jesus brought a great novelty into the world by the mere fact of bringing himself! Revelation and revealer, in Jesus, are the same thing: he who speaks is also he of whom he speaks and this is so because "the Word was God" (John 1:1). We now have a prophetic message that is altogether reliable, to which we do well to be attentive, as to a lamp shining in a dark place (cf. 2 Pet 1:19).

One day, after reading a passage from the prophet Isaiah in the synagogue at Nazareth, Jesus closed the scroll and said, "Today this scripture has been fulfilled" (cf. Luke 4:21). Not only that particular scripture, but all the Scriptures, have been fulfilled in Christ; he is God's yes to all the promises and all the prophecies (cf. 2 Cor 1:19). The Son, through whom God has spoken to us, is "the heir to all things" (cf. Heb 1:2) and, first of all, of those things said under the Old Covenant; he it is who "recapitulates" in himself all the Scriptures. The Lamb who, in the Book of Revelation, advances to receive the book from the hands of him who sits upon the throne, and then breaks open its seals (Rev 5–6), is a plastic image conveying that by his death Jesus has made the book of the Scriptures his own and that only he can completely explain them. The book has become his book; he has inherited it from the Father. All the words of the Law and the Prophets have thus flowed together, like so many drops of water, into the great sea which is the very Word of God, the Son. Paul says that Christ was the term (i.e., the end and the aim) of the Law (cf. Rom 10:4), that everything in the Old Testament was said by allegory, referring forward to Christ (cf. Gal 4:24), for our use who live at the end of the ages (cf. 1 Cor 10:11). But here a great truth blazes forth: the Son does not annul the prophets but fulfills them; the New Testament does not diminish the status of the Old Testament but promotes it, making it pass from "the letter" to "the Spirit," transfiguring it into "a ministry of glory" (cf. 2 Cor 3:7f.). By his death and resurrection, Christ opens the hitherto sealed Old Testament and reveals its true content: "Then," after Easter, "he opened their minds to understand the Scriptures" (Luke 24:45).

The result is that today we hear Christ's voice even when we read the Law, the Prophets, and the Psalms; they "speak of him" (cf. Luke 24:27; John 5:39), and he speaks in them. The liturgy expresses this conviction by having us listen at Mass to one page from the Old Testament and one from the New. St. Ambrose writes:

> Drink from the springs of the Old and New Testaments, since in the one as in the other you drink Christ. . . . Drink Christ, by drinking his words: the Old Testament is his word and the New Testament is his word. The Sacred Scriptures are drunk and the Sacred Scriptures are eaten when the sap of the Eternal Word descends into the veins of the spirit and into the powers of the soul. . . . Drink this word, but drink it in its proper order: first drink it in the Old Testament, then drink it straightway as well in the New.[3]

3. Word-event and Word-sacrament

The author of the Epistle to the Hebrews wrote quite a long time after the death of Jesus, even longer, therefore, after Jesus had begun to speak; and yet we have already heard him say, "God has spoken to us in the Son recently, in these days." He therefore regarded the days in which he was living as being part of the days of Jesus. For this reason, a little further on, and quoting the words of the psalm, "Today if you hear his voice, do not harden your hearts," he applies them to Christians and says, "Take care, brothers, that there be not found among you anyone with a perverse and faithless heart who may forsake the living God; but rather encourage one another every day, as long as this 'today' lasts" (cf. Heb 3:11).

So, even today, God speaks in the Church and speaks "in the Son." But how and where can we listen to "his voice"? Divine revelation is closed: in one sense, there are no more words of God. And here we discover another affinity between Word and Eucharist. The Eucharist is present throughout salvation-history: first in the Old Testament, as type, then in the New Testament as event, and finally in the Church as sacrament. True, Christ's sacrifice was once and for all concluded on the cross; in a certain sense, therefore, there are no more sacrifices for Christ. Yet we know that there is still a sacrifice and that the unique sacrifice of the Cross is made present and operant in the Eucharistic sacrifice; the event continues in the sacrament, and history in the liturgy. Something analogous occurs with the Word of Christ: it has ceased to exist as event but continues to exist as sacrament.

Let me try to explain this. In the Bible, the Word of God (*dabar*), especially in the particular form it takes in the prophets, always constitutes an event; it is a word-event, that is to say a word that creates a situation, that always sets off something new in history. The recurring expression, "the word of Yahweh came to . . ." could be translated as "the word of Yahweh took concrete form in . . ." (in Ezekiel, in Haggai, in Zechariah, etc.).

This type of word-event continues until John the Baptist; indeed in Luke we read: "In the fifteenth year of the reign of Tiberius Caesar . . . the word of God came down (*factum est verbum Domini super*) on John the son of Zechariah in the desert" (cf. Luke 3:1f.). But from this moment the formula disappears from the rest of the Bible and in its place appears another: no longer "Factum est verbum Domini" but "Verbum caro factum est": the Word was made flesh (John 1:14). The word-event gives place to the Word-person. We never encounter the phrase "the word of God came to Jesus," since he is the Word. To the provisional realizations of the Word of God in the prophets there now succeeds full and definitive realization. In a famous passage, St. John of the Cross observes,

11

By giving us his Son, God has spoken to us once and for all and has nothing left to reveal. God has become, as it were, dumb, and has no more to say. . . . Wherefore he that would now enquire of God or seek any vision or revelation, would not only be acting foolishly but would be committing an offence against God, by not setting his eyes altogether upon Christ and seeking no new thing or aught beside. And God might answer him after this manner, saying: "This is my beloved Son, in whom I am well-pleased. Hear ye him. If I have spoken all things to you in my Word, which is my Son, and I have no other word, what answer can I now make to you, or what can I reveal to you which is greater than this? Set your eyes on him alone; in him I have spoken and revealed to you all things; and in him you shall find yet more than that which you ask or desire."[4]

But we have to understand this aright: God has become "dumb" in the sense that he doesn't say anything new regarding what he has said in Jesus, but not in the sense that he no longer speaks; he is forever repeating what he has already said in Jesus!

Jesus is thus the final event of the Word of God in history; he is that word "issuing from the mouth of God" that, like the rain, has come down upon the earth and watered it so it can bear seed to sow and bread to eat, and, once everything has been completed that God sent him to do, returns to him, saying to the Father, "I have accomplished the work you gave me to do" (cf. Isa 15:10f.; John 17:4). The Word's stint in history closes with Christ's ascension into heaven, but the Spirit that was at work in it "lasts forever" (cf. John 14:16); so this too, mysteriously, lasts forever. There will be no more *word-events* in the Church; the Word of God will not come down on anyone again as once it came down on Samuel, Jeremiah, or John the Baptist; but there are *word-sacraments*. Word-sacraments are God's words "come down" once and for all and collected together in the Bible; these become "active reality" each time the Church proclaims them with authority, and the Spirit who inspired them rekindles them in the hearts of those who hear them.

When we speak of the Word as "sacrament," we use the term not in the technical and strict sense of the seven sacraments, but in that wider sense in which we speak of Christ as "the primordial sacrament of the Father" and of the Church as "the universal sacrament of salvation."[5] St. Augustine says that the sacrament is "a word that you see" (*verbum visibile*), and the word "a sacrament that you hear" (*sacramentum audibile*).[6] In every sacrament there is a distinction between the visible sign and the invisible reality, grace. The word we read in the Bible is in itself only a material sign (like water and bread), a collection of dead syllables or, at best, one word among all the rest of the human vocabulary; but, faith and the illumination of the Holy Spirit intervening, by means of such signs we mysteriously enter into contact with the living truth and the will of God. Who has not experienced this at some time or another? Unexpectedly a word of God has, as it were, caught fire for us; we have almost heard God's living voice address our hearts; so clear it sounded as to make us exclaim: This is addressed to me. Yes, I'm the one. My God, you've caught me in the act! This is the miracle of the Word made vehicle for God's power. "Christ's body is not more truly present in the Blessed Sacrament than is Christ's truth in the preaching of the Gospel. In the mystery of the Eucharist, the species that you see are signs, but that which is enclosed in them is the very being of Christ; in Scripture, the words that you hear are signs but the thought that these represent is the very truth of the Son of God" (J.-B. Bossuet). As in the incarnation Jesus hides under the veil of flesh and, in the Eucharist, under the veil of bread, so in Scripture he hides under the veil of speech. In the incarnation, God hides "in the lowliness of human nature"; in Scripture, he hides in the lowliness of human language.

The sacramental nature of the Word of God is shown by the way on occasion it manifestly operates beyond the comprehension of the listener, which comprehension may be limited and imperfect; it operates virtually on its own. When the prophet Elisha told Naaman the Syrian, who had gone to him to be cured of his leprosy, that he should wash seven times in the Jordan, Naaman angrily replied: "Are not the rivers of Damascus, the Abana and the Pharfar, better than all the waters of Israel? Could I not wash in them and be cleansed?" (2 Kgs 5:12). Naaman was right: the rivers of Syria were unquestionably better and had more water in them; yet, by washing in the Jordan he was healed and his flesh became like a little boy's again, something that would never have happened if he had washed in the great rivers of his own country. So it is with the Word of God contained in the Scriptures. In the world at large and even within the Church there have been

13

and there will be better books than some books in the Bible—of greater literary refinement and, religiously speaking, more edifying (suffice it to mention *The Imitation of Christ*)—yet none of these produces the effect that the most modest of the inspired books produces.

In the words of Scripture there is something that acts over and above any human explanation; there is an obvious disproportion between the sign and the reality produced by it, which makes one indeed think of the way the sacraments act. "The waters of Israel," the divinely inspired Scriptures, still cure the leprosy of sin today; the gospel passage for the Mass having been read, the Church invites the minister to kiss the book and say, "May the words of the gospel cancel our sins." In *Tales of a Russian Pilgrim,* we read of many people being cured of the vice of drinking, thanks to their having kept a resolution to read a chapter of the gospel whenever they felt the compulsive need for a drink coming on. Recommending the practice to one such, a monk said: "In the very words of the Gospel there is a life-giving power, for in them is written what God himself has uttered. Never mind if you do not understand it properly; it is enough if you read carefully. If you don't understand the Word of God, the demons certainly do understand what you are reading, and they tremble."[7]

All this has inspired souls in love with the Word of God with a kind of holy reverence for the words of Scripture: "You who are accustomed to take part in divine mysteries know, when you receive the body of the Lord, how you protect it with all caution and veneration, lest any small part fall from it, lest anything of the consecrated gift be lost. For you believe, and correctly, that you are answerable if anything falls from there by neglect. But if you are so careful to preserve his body, and rightly so, how do you think there is less guilt to have neglected God's Word than to have neglected his body?"[8] St. Francis of Assisi, too, united "the most holy mysteries" (i.e., the Eucharist) and "the most holy words" of the Lord in one same tender feeling of affection. In connection with the latter, he once wrote:

> I urge all my friars and I encourage them in Christ to show all possible respect for God's words wherever they may happen to find them in writing. If they are not kept properly or if they lie thrown about disrespectfully, they should pick them up and

14

put them aside, paying honour in his words to God who spoke them. God's words sanctify numerous objects, and it is by the power of the words of Christ that the sacrament of the altar is consecrated.[9]

We should prepare ourselves to administer and receive the Word of God just as we prepare ourselves to administer and receive the Eucharist, by entering beforehand into a supernatural climate of faith and of holy fear of God as we pray and adore the mystery of God hidden in the Word.

There was a day when Jesus "began to preach" and there was another day when, having stopped preaching, "he raised his eyes to heaven and said, 'Father, the hour has come . . . now I am coming to you' " (John 17:1, 13). So, too, for us will come the day when we stop reading the Scriptures and set out for the Father's house; then those who here below have listened to his voice "will enter into his rest" (cf. Heb 4:1f.). Then there will be no more need for lamplight, nor for sunlight, for the Lord God himself will give us light (cf. Rev 22:5).

> Then, when that day comes there will be no more need for lamps; we shall no longer listen to the prophet nor open the book of the Apostle, we shall not require the testimony of John, we shall have no further need even of the Gospel; then all the Scriptures will vanish away, which have blazed like lamps for us in the darkness of this world, for we shall no longer be in darkness. . . . When all these aids are no more, what shall we be able to see? how shall our minds be nourished? how shall our gaze be gladdened? . . . So what shall we see? Let the Gospel tell us: "In the beginning was the Word, and the Word was with God, and the Word was God." You will come to the Fountain by which you have already been slightly bedewed; and that Light, of which hardly one ray, reflected and deflected, struck your heart in the darkness here below, you will see in all its brilliance.[10]

The Scriptures will vanish away and words will cease, but the Word will remain! The Word was in the beginning and at the end, too, will be the Word.

15

NOTES

1. *Sacrosanctum Concilium* 7.
2. St. Augustine, *Tractatus in Iohannis Evangelium* 29.3 (CCL 36, p. 285).
3. St. Ambrose, *In Psalmum Enarratio* 1.33 (PL 14, 983).
4. St. John of the Cross, *Ascent of Mount Carmel* 2.22.4-5.
5. *Lumen gentium* 48.
6. Cf. St. Augustine, *Tractatus in Iohannis Evangelium* 80.3; *Contra Faustum Manichaeum* 19.6.
7. *Tales of a Russian Pilgrim* 2.
8. Origen, *In Exodum homilia* 13.2 (PG 12, 391).
9. St. Francis of Assisi, *Letter to the Chapter General & all the Friars* 4 (St. Francis of Assisi, *Writings and Early Biographies,* Chicago 1973, p. 107).
10. St. Augustine, *Tractatus in Iohannis Evangelium* 35.9 (CCL 36, p. 322).

Chapter II

"GO AND PROCLAIM
THE GOSPEL"

The Word of God in the Church

St. Ephrem the Syrian likens the Word of God to a fountain continuously throwing up water; whoever goes to this fountain draws a little water, enough to quench his or her thirst, and then goes away. But the fountain goes on welling up perpetually, and much more remains than anyone can manage to carry away.

> The Lord has hidden all his treasures in his Word, so that each of us should find something rich in what we contemplate. . . . Having acquired something rich ourselves, we do not suppose there can be nothing else in the Word of God besides what we ourselves have found. On the contrary, we realize we have only been able to discover one thing among many others. Having been enriched by the Word, we do not imagine the Word has been impoverished thereby; unable to exhaust its riches, we give thanks for its immensity. So rejoice that you have been filled, but do not grieve over the fact that the riches of the Word are more than you can absorb.[1]

This image describes our own situation. We have traced the history of the Word, starting from its focal center, which is Christ, and going back from him to the prophets, and flowing forward to the Church. We have seen that, having ceased as event, the Word today exists as sacrament; Scripture, in other words, exists in the Church. This is precisely the fountain where we come henceforth to draw water. St. Ephrem has explained to us that we must abandon any pretensions to exhausting this fountain, taking in every aspect of the Word of God. Instead, we must enter into the state of mind of thirsty pilgrims who go to the fountain, drink what at that moment flows from the fountain, and come away

17

happy in the knowledge that we can always return and always find other water to quench our thirst.

1. *The Church is borne by the Word*

From the spring of Scripture we hear that "All mankind is grass. . . . The grass withers, the flower wilts . . . but the word of our God endures forever" (cf. Isa 40:6-8). According to the First Epistle of Peter, "the word" spoken of in that passage "is the word of the Gospel" (cf. 1 Pet 1:25). And indeed Jesus himself was to say, "Heaven and earth will pass away, but my words will not pass away" (cf. Matt 24:35). In accordance with a transformation of which we are now well aware, the "word of God" has now become "the word of Christ."

But let us see what is entailed in this Word, this solemn *dabar* of God. In Deutero-Isaiah (whose "call" the text cited above describes), we constantly find the conviction that "Israel depends in all things and for all things on the Word of God" (G. von Rad). The same idea is expressed in Deuteronomy when Moses says to the people, "This word is your life" (cf. Deut 32:47). Israel feels itself as it were "borne" by the Word of God; when all resources fail during the Exile, the Word appears as the unique support, as the power "eternally resisting" amid the fluctuations of human affairs, as the rock on which Israel's house is built.

Today all this is true for the new Israel, the Church, which has her foundations in the Word of Jesus: "This Son . . . sustains all things by his mighty word" (or "by the power of his word") says the passage in the Epistle to the Hebrews on which we have already commented (Heb 1:3). The Church is truly "the house built on the rock" (cf. Matt 7:25), and the rock is the Word. The Word, here, means something more than the entire sum of the words of God; it is a creative power acting in history and opposing the fleeting powers of human beings that "will pass away." It is a living reality; it is presented as such in the Acts of the Apostles, where it is said that "the Word grew," "continued to spread," "gained influence and power" (cf. Acts 6:7; 12:24; 19:20); and St. Paul depicts it in the same way when he writes that it "sounds forth" like a mighty shout through all Macedonia and Achaia (cf. 1 Thess 1:8).

When the New Testament states that Christians have been "born anew through the living and abiding Word of God" (cf. 1 Pet 1:23; Jas 1:18), this means they have begun living in contact with this mysterious force, which is the Word. "And such is the force and power of the Word of God that it can serve the Church as her support and vigor, and the children of the Church as strength for their faith, food for the soul, and a pure and lasting fount of spiritual life."[2] This way of thinking about the Word, in its dimension of life-giving mystery, is close to that of the Fathers: "The Word of God," says St. Ambrose, "is the vital sustenance of the soul; it feeds it, pastures it, and guides it; nothing can keep the human soul alive except the Word of God."[3]

In ancient times, in the back part of the tent or holy of holies (called *debir*), were the "ten Words" (*debarim*), kept in the ark; these constituted the deepest secret in the history of the chosen people. Now, in the new Israel, this deep secret, this nucleus from which all sprouts, this center of expansion hidden in the Church's heart, is the Word and the Eucharist together, the Word made Bread which yet is forever the Word.

2. The Church bears the Word

And this is exactly where we discover the other face of the mystery: the Church is borne by the Word, but also bears the Word. The Church is the new ark of the covenant, keeping "the words" safe. And, once again, the Church imitates Mary, who after the incarnation bore the Word in her womb and was borne by the Word.

Speaking of the Church as bearing the Word means speaking about Tradition, the entrusting (*traditio*) that Christ made to the Church when, ascending into heaven, he said to the apostles, "Go into the whole world and proclaim the gospel to every creature" (Mark 16:15). St. Paul justifies his preaching on these very grounds: "The gospel preached by me . . . I received from Jesus Christ" (cf. Gal 1:11f.). Before being the Tradition that the apostles transmitted to the Church (Tradition in the active sense), the apostolic Tradition was the Tradition the apostles received from Christ (Tradition in the passive sense). In this first passing— from Jesus to the apostles—lies the true nature of Tradition; it is not a second source of revelation containing things different from and additional to Scripture; at its deepest, it is no other than Scripture itself as understood and taught in the Church and by the Church. A conciliar text says that "sacred Tradition and sacred Scripture make up a single sacred deposit of the Word of God."[4] The apostolic Tradition—as Irenaeus, Origen and other great figures of the past have conceived it—is "the understanding, or meaning, attached to the Scriptures by the Church." The bread of life (i.e., the Word of God), says one Father, comes to us as if it were already chopped up and chewed by the teeth of the apostolic Tradition.[5]

So Tradition is not something static and dead, but something very much alive. A living reality, such as the Word of God, cannot be kept alive in dead surroundings. St. Irenaeus writes that revealed truth, "like a precious liquor contained in a costly vessel, by the activity of the Spirit of God is forever renewed and likewise renews the vessel that contains it," which is the Church's proclamation and the apostolic tradition.[6] Outside the living environment of Tradition, the Scriptures would be a dead body, a book like any other, however sublime, to be studied with all the rigor of the historico-philological method and nothing more (as indeed is the case today where they are studied in environments in which the Church's faith exerts no influence).

But keeping the Word of God alive is not a mere right or privilege of the Church; above all, it is a duty, a responsibility. Like St. Paul, the Church must say, "If I preach the gospel, this is no reason for me to boast, for an obligation has been imposed on me, and woe to me if I do not preach it! . . . I have been entrusted with a stewardship" (1 Cor 9:16-17).

One of Charles Péguy's characters, personifying Mother Church, speaks as follows to a little girl representing the average Christian:

> Jesus did not give us dead words
> for us to salt away in little tins
> (or big ones),
> for us to preserve in rancid oil.
> Jesus Christ, my girl,
> did not give us word-pickles
> to keep.

No, he gave us living words
to feed. . . .
The words of life,
the living words can only be preserved alive. . . .
On us, weak creatures of flesh, it depends
to keep these words uttered alive in time alive,
to feed them and keep them alive in time.
Mystery of mysteries,
we have been given this privilege,
this excessive, unbelievable privilege,
of preserving the words of life alive. . . .
We are called to feed the word of the Son of God.
Oh penury, oh calamity,
it falls to our lot,
our duty it is, on us it depends
to make it heard forever and ever,
to make it ring out. . . .[7]

It isn't hard to guess what is meant by salting the words away "in little tins," keeping them "in rancid oil," or "letting them go moldy," since, alas, we are familiar with such things from experience. They are what happens when the Word is denied the opportunity of moving about and circulating, of breaking off and crying out, of tearing down and building up—as is in its nature—but is kept as it were under a glass dome, in an antiseptic environment, under strict control, sliced up, as often as not, into so many little phrases or disconnected quotations; for in this way it can be tamed, its dangerous strength canalized into theological theses or practical decisions, where it is used more or less as an excipient or as a straitjacket.

3. *Servants of the Word*

The apostles taught the Church once and for all how to obviate this risk by declaring themselves and their successors to be "servants of the Word" (cf. Luke 1:2; Acts 6:4; Rom 1:1). This title has first and foremost a dogmatic bearing; it means, as *Dei Verbum* explains, that

the task of giving an authentic interpretation of the Word of God, whether in its written form or in the form of Tradition, has been entrusted to the living teaching office of the Church alone. Its authority in this matter is exercised in the name of Jesus Christ. Yet this Magisterium is not superior to the Word of God, but is its servant. It teaches only what has been handed on to it. At the divine command and with the help of the Holy Spirit, it listens to this devotedly, guards it with dedication and expounds it faithfully.[8]

But "the service of the Word" also has an ascetic and spiritual dimension: it postulates certain concrete spiritual attitudes in those who are to proclaim the Word. The first of these attitudes is *consistency between the Word proclaimed and the life of the proclaimer*. This is the first and fundamental way of serving the Word: being at its service, obeying it in one's own life. "Servants of the Word" means people who obey the Word! We find two kinds of preachers described in the New Testament. To the first belong the scribes and Pharisees, of whom Jesus says, "Do and observe all things whatsoever they tell you, but do not follow their example. For they preach but they do not practice. They tie up heavy burdens and lay them on people's shoulders, but they will not lift a finger to move them" (Matt 23:3-4).

To the second kind of preacher belongs, in pride of place, that same Jesus who can in all truth say, "Learn from me . . ." (Matt 11:29). "I have given you a model to follow, so that as I have done for you, you should also do" (John 13:15). To it also belongs the apostle Paul who can say to his hearers, "Be imitators of me, as I am of Christ" (1 Cor 11:1; cf. Phil 3:17).

Preachers who hold out a fine ideal of life yet live the very opposite themselves, who recommend "the narrow way" to others but follow a broader way themselves, are like marine architects who have built a magnificent ship but, when the time comes to launch her and venture out onto the open sea, choose not to go aboard but follow at a distance in a lifeboat. People won't be easily persuaded to take passage in that ship!

People have learned to mistrust mere words, since they have so often been deceived by them, or have deceived others with them. When, however, they encounter individuals utterly committed to what they preach, suffering or actually dying for it, this makes a big impression; from experience everyone knows people are only prepared to suffer for things they really believe in. This being so, "the lived Word" has uniquely, irreplaceably persuasive force. It convinces! It also convinces because the word we have already experienced and suffered in our own life and in our own prayer-life issues from our lips with a quite special passion and vehemence. In it there is a particle of the proclaimer's own soul, and this seizes on the soul of the listener. Existential, not merely conceptual, communication occurs.

Preaching is easy enough; practicing is the hard part. A saint very dear to the Russian people, St. Serafim of Sarov, used to say that preaching is as easy as throwing stones from the top of a church-tower, whereas putting into practice is as hard as carrying stones to the top of the tower on your back. Ideally we should only throw those stones we have manhandled up the tower in the first place, or in other words, preach only what we have already put into practice. But such perfect consistency between the Word and life is pretty rare; what is more, those who possess it are the last to perceive it. Meanwhile, the Word of God cannot wait. So what is to be done? Should one keep quiet? St. Paul's words cheer us on: "We do not preach ourselves but Jesus Christ as Lord" (2 Cor 4:5). The Word is true, not for the life of the preacher but for the life of Christ, who has fulfilled every word of the gospel. We ought to sink into the dust for shame at the distance that separates us from the Word, but even so we cannot keep silent about the Word, and there lies our punishment and humiliation.

Where, then, this consistency of life is not to be found, *humility* must take its place. This is the second attitude of spirit needed for being "servants of the Word": to disappear in the presence of the Word, to renounce one's own glory. The true "servant of the Word" is the one who thinks, like John the Baptist: "I am the voice of someone crying" (cf. John 1:23). What, St. Augustine wonders, is the task of the voice? It is, so to speak, that of taking the word or the thought that is in my heart and of conveying it on the wave of a breath through the air to the ear of the brother standing before me. Once this task has been completed, the voice has finished its job; it must fall silent, die away, while the word makes its regal entry into my brother's heart to take up its dwelling there and bear fruit. The "voice" says: "This, the Word, must increase whereas I must decrease" (cf. John 3:30); the preacher says, "He, Jesus, must grow and I must vanish."

23

The Church does precisely this when, drawing the Word from her "bosom" where it is kept, she cries it on the housetops so that it may reach the ears and hearts of all people and all may believe and be saved. For the hierarchy of the Church, to be "the servant of the Word" means not to want to be the Word, but only the voice of the Word. It means, as St. Paul appositely observes, not preaching oneself but Christ Jesus as Lord.

4. *"But the Word of God is not chained!"*

To bear the Word therefore, the Church must at once be consistent and humble. But she also has to be simple and poor. The apostle Paul exhorted the Christians of Thessalonica to pray, so that the Word of the Lord might be able "to run its course to the end" (cf. 2 Thess 3:1; this is the literal translation of the Greek). The image suggests a sort of race of the Word, from Jerusalem to Rome, and thereafter from the center of the Church out into the world. To be able to complete such a race, the Word should not find too many obstacles in its path; it should be free and naked, like an athlete.

At this point I can't help thinking of a story by Kafka which strikes me as a perfect parable for the Church. It is common knowledge that this author's stories are often religiously inspired and powerfully symbolic, and this story is certainly an example of this. It is short enough to quote in its entirety:

> The emperor, they say, has sent you a message; yes, you personally, miserable subject, insignificant shadow cowering from the imperial sun at the back of beyond; the emperor from his deathbed has sent a message to you alone. He made the messenger kneel down beside the bed and whispered the message in his ear; he set so much store by the contents that he made the messenger whisper it back to him. With a nod of his head he confirmed the accuracy of the words. And before those who were present at his death—all obstructing walls have been dismantled; on broad and lofty staircases, the grandees of the empire stand round—in the presence of all he dismissed the messenger. The messenger set out at once: a vigorous, tireless man. Swinging now one arm, now the other, he opens a path through the crowd; if he encounters resistance, he points to his chest which displays the device of the sun; and so he goes for-

ward, as easily as you please. But the crowd is immense, its lodgings vast. How easily he would fly if he had free passage! Very soon you would hear the glorious hammering of his fists on your door. Instead, he strives in vain; he goes on forcing his way through the rooms of the inner palace, from which he will never emerge. But even if he did, it wouldn't be any use: he would have to struggle down the steps. And even if he managed to do that, he still wouldn't have achieved anything: he would still have to cross the courtyards; and after the courtyards, the second circle of palaces; and more flights of steps and courtyards, another palace and so on, for thousands of years. Eventually he manages to rush out through the final gate—but this can never, never happen—and lo, before him lies the imperial city, the centre of the world, piled high with mountains of its own rubbish. There, through that, no one can make headway, not even with a dead man's message. You meanwhile sit at your window and dream about that message, as evening falls.[9]

What things are evoked by those "mountains of rubbish" in the midst of the city of the king! From his deathbed, on the cross, our King entrusted a message to his Church, and every day, in the Eucharistic sacrifice, he whispers it to us again: "Tell the world that I love it and am dying for its sins! Tell the world that joy is possible!" There are still so many people, far away, who, standing at the window, dream of a message such as this. It is essential that the Church never become that complicated, suffocating castle from which the message can no longer get out but that, as it was in the beginning, at the moment the King was dying, "all obstructing walls be dismantled."

St. Paul wrote to Timothy: "I am suffering, even to the point of chains, . . . but the Word of God is not chained" (2 Tim 2:9). He meant that the important thing is that the Word of God should not be chained; nothing else matters. The Church may be chained by persecution, by suffering, by her own weakness. There is no particular impediment in this; such things often make proclamation run the faster. It is other things that put the brakes on the race of the Word, such as an excess of human resources and of reliance on human resources, the too many jackets and too many knapsacks that weigh down the messenger, to use Jesus' own words (cf. Luke 10:4); the quest for one's own glory is the most pernicious of riches. Other impediments may be an excess of bureaucracy; a clericalism that takes the bite out of the Word and makes it seem remote from life; and a plethora of abstruse, incomprehensible lingo. All of these are unduly prudent, self-defensive attitudes that make us keep our portcullises lowered. To this situation, too, can the words of the psalm be applied: "Lift up, O gates, your lintels; reach up, you ancient portals . . ." (Ps 24:7). Let the world throw wide its gates to let Christ *in,* and the Church throw hers wide to let Christ *out!*

What we read in Manzoni's great novel, *The Betrothed,* about Perpetua's secret comes to mind. This lady knows about something amazing that has happened in the district. All circumstances concur that the news should be kept hidden but, however hard she tries, she cannot manage it. "A great big secret like that in the poor woman's heart was like very new wine in an old, badly hooped cask, fermenting and gurgling and bubbling up, just not blowing out the cork, but swishing round inside, and coming frothing or seeping out between the staves, or dribbling out in sufficient quantities here and there for people to taste it and tell more or less what wine it was."[10] The good news of the kingdom should be, in the Church and in the heart of the individual Christian, exactly like new wine in the wineskin or the cask and like that secret in the woman's heart: so impelling and so lovely that it cannot be kept hidden but trickles out, as it were, from every pore. "What you hear whispered," says Jesus, "proclaim on the housetops" (Matt 10:27).

NOTES

1. St. Ephrem the Syrian, *Commentary on the Diatessaron* 1.18–19 (SCh 121, p. 52f.).
2. *Dei Verbum* 21.
3. St. Ambrose, *In Psalmum Expositio* 118.7.7 (PL 15, 1350).
4. *Dei Verbum* 10.
5. Gregory of Elvira, *Tractatus Origenis* 6 (CCL 69, 55).
6. St. Irenaeus, *Adversus Haereses* 3.24.1.
7. Charles Péguy, "Le porche du mystère de la deuxième vertu," in *Oeuvres poétiques* (Paris, 1957) 586–88.
8. *Dei Verbum* 10.
9. Franz Kafka, "An Imperial Message," in *Stories.*
10. Alessandro Manzoni, *The Betrothed,* chap. 11.

Chapter III

"WHEN I FOUND YOUR WORDS . . ."

The Word in the life of the proclaimer

In our first meditation we saw that even the Old Testament is a book about Christ, which he "inherited," along with everything else, from the Father. It is most important to keep this truth before our eyes, especially in the present meditation, where we have to keep passing from the Old Testament to the New.

In the First Book of Kings we read of Elijah's encounter with God on Horeb. Fleeing from the wrath of Ahab and Jezebel, Elijah reaches Horeb, the mountain of God. There he goes into a cave to spend the night, "but the Word of the Lord came to him, 'Why are you here, Elijah?' He answered, 'I have been most zealous for the Lord of hosts but the Israelites have forsaken your covenant'. . . . Then the Lord said, 'Go outside and stand on the mountain before the Lord.' " There then takes place that mysterious theophany we know so well; there was a "tempestuous wind," but the Lord was not in the wind; there was "an earthquake" but the Lord was not in the earthquake; there was "a fire" but the Lord was not in the fire. After the fire there was "a tiny whispering sound" and in the tiny whispering sound was the Lord (cf. 1 Kgs 19:1-13).

This is a very evocative episode, but it must not be misunderstood, as it frequently is. It does not mean that the Word of God always manifests itself as a gentle whisper and has nothing in common with the wind, the earthquake, and the fire. On the contrary, it is all these things, as can be seen in the life of Elijah himself. Ben-Sira, pronouncing his eulogy of Elijah, says, "Like a fire there appeared the prophet Elijah, whose words were like a flaming furnace" (cf. Sir 48:1). The lesson to be learned from the episode concerns, rather, the way the prophet receives the Word of

God. The prophet, for his part, calmly and in silence accepts the Word, but within him it is transformed, and it pours out on the people in the form of fire and thunder. Elijah is the prototype and symbol of those who proclaim the Word of God. Setting out from his experience, let us try in this meditation to illuminate that personal relationship between the Word and the prophet, between *listening to* and *proclaiming* the Word.

1. The Word issuing from silence

The episode we have recalled unfolds in a very particular atmosphere: at night, in the desert, on the mountain, in great silence and deep solitude. People have been left behind, far away; here there are only the Lord and his angel (the one who says to Elijah, "Get up and eat"). And indeed one does have to journey afar and enter the kingdom of silence before one can hear the Word "that issues from the mouth of God." In this respect, Elijah did indeed—in spirit—come back to life in John the Baptist, for on John the Baptist, too, "the Word of God came down in the desert" (cf. Luke 3:2). If words of God are few and far between, this is because there is too little silence. The Word of God always issues from silence: this is the condition of its "virginity." St. Ignatius of Antioch said that Jesus Christ was "the Word of the Father issuing from silence."[1] Similarly, once the Word had come on earth, when he "began to preach," his word issued from the silence, the great silence of Nazareth. Just as before receiving the Eucharist we have to fast from food and drink, so too we have to fast before receiving the Word: fast from our own and other people's words. So great is the insistence of the Word of God on being kept distinct from human words that, sending out his disciples to preach the gospel, Jesus advised them to "greet no one along the way" (Luke 10:4).

But it is not merely a matter of silence, at least not merely of exterior silence; rather it is a matter of a total emptying of self, of being "set apart for the gospel," set apart from all, as the Apostle says of himself (cf. Rom 1:1). It is like advancing into a desert, jettisoning, the farther we advance into it, mental pictures, images, memories, desires, and idols of the clamorous world we have left behind. The Word of God on this occasion ("Go,

28

anoint Hazael, anoint Jehu, anoint Elisha'') reached Elijah at the end of a desolate road, when his strength was exhausted and he was so convinced he had failed that he exclaimed, "This is enough, O LORD! Take my life, for I am no better than my fathers" (1 Kgs 19:4). The earthen vessel must first be completely emptied, before it can receive the treasure of the Word of God (cf. 2 Cor 4:7). "Suppose," St. Augustine says, "God wanted to fill you with honey; if you are full of vinegar, where will you put the honey? The contents of the vessel will have to be thrown away, and the vessel will have to be washed immediately, painstakingly washed and scoured, so as to be fit to receive this mysterious gift."[2] Would you proclaim the Word of God? You must go each time and take it from the arms of the Crucified, on the cross.

Seemingly the Word of God is within arm's reach; it is at hand in the Scriptures. But in fact it is like those alpine flowers that grow on jagged and precipitous rocks: one has to tear one's hands and fingers to go and pick them. For the would-be proclaimer, Scripture becomes that desert in which we wander bewildered like Elijah. This was long ago observed by Origen, who possibly knew the Scriptures better than anyone else before or since. Before deriving nourishment from them, he said, one has to endure a certain "poverty of the senses"; the soul is surrounded by darkness on every side and keeps encountering paths with no way out. Then, suddenly, after painful search and prayer, lo and behold, the voice of the Word rings out and immediately everything is light; the One sought by the soul comes to meet her, "springing across the mountains, leaping across the hills" (cf. Cant 2:8), that is to say opening the mind to receive a strong and luminous word from him.[3]

2. The book at once sweet and sour

Great is the joy at the moment of meeting between proclaimer and the Word; it is proportionate to the trouble endured in research and in waiting. Jeremiah describes this unique moment as follows: "When I found your words, I devoured them; they became my joy and the happiness of my heart" (Jer 15:16).

Scripture uses the same image several times to describe this moment when God gives his word to the human soul: the image of the "little book" offered to be eaten. Implicitly it is already present in the passage from Jeremiah I have just quoted. In Ezekiel we read:

> I saw a hand stretched out to me, in which was a written scroll which he unrolled before me. It was covered with writing front and back, and written on it was: Lamentation and wailing and woe! He said to me, "Son of man, . . . eat this scroll, then go, speak to the house of Israel." So I opened my mouth and he gave me the scroll to eat. "Son of man," he then said to me, "feed your belly and fill your stomach with this scroll I am giving you." I ate it, and it was as sweet as honey in my mouth (Ezek 2:9–3:3).

This image recurs in the Book of Revelation, but here an important element has been added: the "little book" is indeed "as sweet as honey" in the mouth, but it turns the prophet's stomach sour (cf. Rev 10:8-10). Here the book represents the concrete message the prophet is called to proclaim on a particular occasion, but clearly it also represents the Word of God in general; it expresses a constant rule in serving the Word. We must try to grasp the image of the scroll, for it says more about the service of the Word than entire treatises on how to proclaim it.

God says to the prophet, "Take and eat this scroll, gobble it up, swallow it." There is a huge difference between simply reading or studying a book, and swallowing it. In the first case, the book remains outside; the relationship with the Word is mediated and detached. The Word has only passed by way of the eyes or the brain of the proclaimer; a sort of simple decanting takes place, from the pages of books to the ears of the listeners (or to the pages of other books, should we be dealing with written proclamation). "He speaks like a printed book," one says of such a proclaimer. He is hard put to it to move his hearers' hearts.

In the second case—the swallowed book—the Word becomes "incarnate" in the proclaimer, becomes "word made flesh," a living, efficacious word. The relationship between proclaimer and Word is immediate and personal. There is a sort of mysterious identification, which gives one indeed to think (by analogy, of course) of the incarnation. Proclaimers who swallow the Word and welcome it into their belly, as Mary did, allow the Word of God to become incarnate again and to "dwell among men." The

30

Word swallowed is a Word assimilated by a human being, even though this is a passive assimilation (as in the case of the Eucharist); the proclaimer is in a state of "being assimilated" by the Word, subjugated and overcome by it as the more powerful vital principle.

But let us enter into the heart of the image. The little book, Revelation says, is as sweet as honey in the mouth but extremely sour in the stomach. What does this mean? That the Word is sweet for other people, for the ones who hear it from our lips, but sour for the proclaimer; indeed, the sweeter and more persuasive it may be for others, the more sour it has been for us. "With regard to our ministry," says the Apostle to his converts in Corinth, "death is at work in us, but life in you" (2 Cor 4:12).

3. "You are the one!"

There are two reasons for this sourness; to understand what they are is to penetrate the very depths of the mystery of proclamation. The first is sin. The Word judges sin and we are sinners! (One may object that Jesus wasn't a sinner. This is true, but he bore the sins of all of us and was therefore as though he had committed them himself; hence, more than simply a sinner, he was—as Scripture says—sin [2 Cor 5:21]. But let us respectfully leave Jesus out of this since he is a completely different case, and concentrate on ourselves.) To swallow the scroll full of woe, lamentation, and wailing is to swallow the terrible judgement of God against sin. When this judgement comes in contact with sin, a tremendous struggle breaks out. And this contact occurs, primarily, in the heart of the proclaimer; that is where the tempest must break, otherwise nothing will happen and the Word will reach our lips as a spent force. When the Word of God came to Isaiah, the prophet thought himself a lost soul and exclaimed "Woe is me, I am doomed! For I am a man of unclean lips" (Isa 6:5). The Apostle Paul said that Christ came into the world to save sinners, of whom he, Paul, was the foremost (cf. 1 Tim 1:15). Am I perhaps better than the Apostle Paul? Indeed not! So, I too must say, "of whom I am the foremost!"

St. James speaks of the Word of God as being like a mirror (cf. Jas 1:23). With respect to this, the first malfeasance (there

31

are others too, as we shall shortly see) is that—peculiar to us preachers—of holding up the mirror to our brothers and sisters so that they can look at themselves in it, while we shelter safely behind it. Our clerical mentality instinctively makes us assume that we and the mirror are all one; every word is applied to other people, diverted on to them. The Bible says that the Word of God is "a two-edged sword." "Two-edged" means that it cuts upwards and downwards, but it can also be taken to mean that it cuts backwards and forwards: that it judges not only those who listen to it but those who proclaim it. St. Augustine says, "He is a vain preacher of the Word of God without, who is not himself a listener within." "You," he continues, "are the hearers of the Word, we the preachers. But, within, where no one can see, we are all hearers."[4]

Each time, O preacher of the Word, you inveigh against some sin, each time you expound the parable of the good Samaritan and talk about the priest and Levite who pass by on the other side, each time you find yourself discoursing on the servant who was forgiven a large sum of money but could not bring himself to forgive his fellow-servant, listen carefully and within you you will hear, in your "belly," like an echo to your words, Nathan's denunciation of David: "You are the one! You are the one!' "

We ministers of the Word are in constant danger: in expounding the Word of God, we try till we are red in the face to convince the faithful that it applies to them, actually to them and no one else, without realizing that we are, as it were, skipping the first link in the chain and that everything is hanging in the void. For it is to "us" that it applies! I am standing here shouting, "You are the one!" In so doing, I attract that accusation of Jesus': "Woe to you, scribes and Pharisees, who lay unbearable burdens on other people's shoulders without lifting a finger to help them" (cf. Matt 23:4). Even as I stand here, lo, the Word makes its voice heard within me saying: "Look out! You are the one now! You are the one putting unbearable burdens on other people's shoulders, you are asking for absolute consistency between proclamation and life, even though you are aware of being far removed from that yourself!" I had an important preaching engagement once (I was going to preach my first Lent to the pontifical household) and while reciting my office in the train I found myself saying Psalm 50:

But to the wicked God says:
   "Why do you recite my commandments
   and profess my covenant with your lips?
You hate discipline;
   you cast my words behind you! . . .
I accuse you, I lay the charge before you."

How sour yet salutary were these words to my stomach! Before I could preach the Word to others, the Word preached to me. And how it preached! I was, no doubt of it, that sinner who always has God's statutes and covenant in his mouth but does not care to experience his discipline, who shrinks from needful austerity and evades the Word's radical demands.

Nor is this the only text for a preacher's examination of conscience. St. Paul makes a long indictment of those (in the context, the Jews) who, having had the Scriptures entrusted to them, use them only for passing judgement on others, but not on themselves. You, he says, pride yourself on knowing the will of God and on knowing the difference between right and wrong; you are confident of being a guide to the blind and a light to those in darkness, a trainer to the ignorant and a teacher to the simple, because you possess the Law. Very well, then, you who teach others, why on earth do you not teach yourself? (cf. Rom 2:17-24). The Apostle then offers several examples, but we can give our own: You who condemn hatred and preach love, do you honestly love your neighbor? Do you love your enemies? You who proclaim, "Blessed are the poor," are you truly detached from things, from reward? Are you ready to forsake all? Are you poor?

Lord, now we praise your Word; let us realize with wonder that your Word truly is that two-edged sword which penetrates even between soul and spirit, between joints and marrow and from which no creature can hide (cf. Heb 4:12-13). "The one struck down by your wrath will give you glory, the survivors of fury will keep your festivals" (cf. Ps 77:11).

4. *Sharers in a divine Passion*

But sinfulness is only the first reason for the sourness of the Word of God for the proclaimer. There is another one: but of this I am very hesitant to speak; it would be better in fact if only

33

the saints were to speak of it who have lived it. I speak of it from hearsay, clinging closer than ever to Scripture and speaking "as with God's own words."

That little book first swallowed by Jeremiah, then by Ezekiel, then by John, was full of "lamentation, wailing, and woe." But these lamentations are not in the main human ones; they are God's lament. It rings out, for those who can hear it, all through the Bible, in the cry, "My people, my people!" This wailing is God's secret lamentation over his children who rebel "with continuous rebellion"; it is finally externalized in the tears Christ weeps over Jerusalem. Oh, this is a far deeper cause for bitterness! This is sharing in the *pathos,* the passion, of God. Origen has bequeathed us this profoundly beautiful passage:

> The Savior came down to earth out of compassion for the human race. He underwent our sufferings before he endured the cross, even before he deigned to take our flesh: for, if he had not undergone them beforehand, he would not have come to share our human life with us. What was this suffering that, from the beginning, he underwent for our sake? It was the passion of love. But the Father, the God of the universe, he who is full of forbearance, mercy, and pity, cannot suffer, surely? But perhaps you do not know that, when concerned with human affairs, he endures a human passion? . . . He endures a passion of love.[5]

God the Father endures a passion of love for the human race. The entire Word of God is impregnated with this passion; therefore it cannot be proclaimed coldly, without sharing to some extent in this passion, without being, like Elijah, "most zealous for the Lord of hosts." This is why the word of Elijah, of Jeremiah, of Francis of Assisi, and of so many other saints burned like fire; they had leaned over the abyss, they had glimpsed the truth of a God to whom his creatures will not listen, a Father who is spurned by his children, who is "forced" to go against his inclinations which are only to love and love, and instead is obliged to threaten and threaten, and to punish and punish.

Before Jesus, the man who most nearly lived this "passion of God" was probably the prophet Jeremiah, who in many respects, in any case, prefigured the passion of Christ. At a certain moment, his heart became fused with God's heart, became one heart: then the cry, at once divine and human, anticipating Jesus' in Gethsemane: "My breast, my breast! How I suffer! The walls of my heart! My heart beats wildly; I cannot be silent. . . . The anger of the Lord brims up inside me, I can no longer keep it in" (cf. Jer 4:19; 6:11).

When John had swallowed the little book and once the sourness in his stomach had been soothed away, he heard a word that said, Go, "you must prophesy again about many peoples, nations . . . and kings" (Rev 10:11).

NOTES

1. St. Ignatius of Antioch, *Epistola ad Magnesios* 7.2.
2. St. Augustine, *In Epistolam Iohannis tractatus* 4.6 (PL 35, 2009).
3. Cf. Origen, *In Matthaeum Sermo* 38 (GCS, 1933, p. 7); *In Canticum canticorum* 3 (GCS, 1925, p. 202).
4. St. Augustine, *Sermo* 179.1.7 (PL 38, 966f.).
5. Origen, *In Ezechielem homilia* 6.6 (GCS, 1925, p. 384f.).

Chapter IV

"WE PREACH CHRIST JESUS AS LORD"

The content of Christian preaching

In the Second Epistle to the Corinthians—which is *par excellence* the letter devoted to the ministry of preaching—St. Paul sets out his policy in these words: "We do not preach ourselves but Jesus Christ as Lord!" (2 Cor 4:5). To those same Christians in Corinth in a previous letter he had written: "We proclaim Christ crucified" (1 Cor 1:23). Whenever the Apostle wants to sum up the content of Christian preaching in a single word, the word is invariably the same one; it is a person, Jesus Christ! Of him Paul stresses on the one hand the event of the cross ("Christ crucified"), and on the other the condition into which, thanks to the cross and resurrection, he has entered (i.e., his lordship). But he is always concerned with the same personal reality, seen dynamically, in the successive moments of Christ's existence.

In these affirmations by the Apostle, Jesus is no longer seen—as he was in the gospels—as proclaimer, but as the one proclaimed. A transition has occurred from "Jesus preaching" to "Jesus preached," and this coincides with the transition from the age of Jesus to the age of the Church. Easter reveals who Jesus is; he establishes the kingdom of God by means of the mystery of his death and resurrection, so that in their preaching the apostles can, quite unaffectedly, replace the expression "kingdom of God" with that of "Jesus is Lord." The fundamental nucleus of Jesus' preaching in the gospels was, "The kingdom of God is at hand. Repent and believe in the gospel" (Mark 1:15); the same nucleus and the same scheme (a notice and a command) is to be found, after Pentecost, in the preaching of the apostles, but in this new form: "God has made Jesus both Lord and Messiah. Repent and believe" (cf. Acts 2:36, 38; 3:18f.; 5:31).

36

Parallel with this we see that the expression "gospel of Jesus" acquires a new meaning without, however, losing any of the old; from the subjective meaning of "good news brought by Jesus" (Jesus being the subject), we pass to the objective meaning of "good news concerning Jesus" (Jesus being the object). And this is the meaning the word *gospel* has in the solemn introduction to the Epistle to the Romans: "Paul, a slave of Christ Jesus, called to be an apostle and set apart for the gospel of God, which he promised previously . . . in the holy Scriptures, the gospel about his Son, descended from David according to the flesh, but established as Son of God in power according to the Spirit of holiness through resurrection from the dead, Jesus Christ our Lord" (Rom 1:1-4).

In any case, there is no division or antithesis between Jesus preaching and Jesus preached, between the Jesus of the gospels and the Jesus of the Church, or—as for some time it has been usual to say—between the Jesus of history and the Christ of faith. In his speeches, St. Peter states emphatically that God has made Lord and Messiah that very Jesus whom human beings crucified, that very Jesus who had passed through Galilee healing everyone (cf. Acts 2:36; 10:38f.), not another Jesus, a Jesus created by the Church's faith (as Bultmann was to maintain). Between the gospel preached by Jesus and the gospel preached by the apostles there is no gap, only continuity, since the apostles preached the gospel "in the Holy Spirit" (1 Pet 1:12), that is, since they preached under the guidance of that same Spirit which inspired Jesus to speak. For the Spirit that, at Pentecost, comes on the Church is the same Spirit that, in the Jordan, consecrated Jesus of Nazareth to carry the good news to the poor, that guided his steps and inspired his every action.

After that first Easter, therefore, it is not only a Jesus preached (as a passive object) who is spoken of; it is also a Jesus "subject," a Jesus still preaching, even if he no longer speaks through his own flesh but through his Spirit, since he no longer lives "according to the flesh" but "according to the Spirit." In Jesus, and in Jesus only, is there perfect correspondence between the subject and the object of the preaching, he being at once divine and human. The modern science of communications has coined the catchphrase, "The medium is the message." The phrase is fulfilled to perfection in Christ alone: in him the messenger is the message and the revealer is the revelation.

37

1. *"At the resurrection from the dead"*

The great change from the age of Jesus preaching to the age of Jesus preached occurred, St. Paul says, "at the resurrection from the dead," when Jesus was established as "Son of God in power" (Rom 1:4). Jesus was always Son of God, but he had been this in powerlessness, humility, and suffering; now, however, he is this "in power," with authority, since on him has been conferred all power in heaven and on earth (cf. Matt 28:18). When the faith of the Church wanted to portray the living likeness of this Jesus for its devotion, the famous icon of Christ in Majesty was born, serene of face and, with divine authority, holding the book of his gospel open to the world.

In Jesus came to pass what had happened "in type" in the life of the prophet Jeremiah. One day Jeremiah received a command from God to take a scroll and in it record all the words he had said touching Jerusalem, Judea, and all the nations. The prophet obeyed and sent the scroll to the priests and leaders of the people, so that they could hear the Lord's voice and repent of their ways. They, however, took counsel together and after much discussion persuaded the king to burn the scroll piece by piece in his audience-chamber, saying (as Caiaphas said in the Sanhedrin): "If we let this man go on, the king of Babylon will come and lay our country waste." So the scroll was thrown into the king's brazier. But God intervened again, ordering the prophet to take another scroll and in it write every word he wrote on the first one and others more terrible still, and to keep it in a safe place until everything written in it was completely fulfilled (cf. Jer 36). Thus it befalls in the life of Jesus. The gospel is the scroll dictated by God through his Son Jesus; human beings "erased" the scroll and tried to destroy it by nailing him to the cross. But God has rewritten it from start to finish, in stronger terms than before, by raising Jesus from the dead, and no one henceforth can lay hands on this scroll, "until all shall be accomplished."

Everything, therefore, starts from the resurrection. At his resurrection—when the Spirit bursts into the tomb—the name of Jesus becomes charged with power and splendor, as our sun, in the initial explosion from which the cosmos came into existence, became charged with an energy allowing it to warm the earth till the end of time. But unlike the physical energy hidden in the sun and the entire universe, the spiritual energy hidden in Christ Jesus is not subject to the law of entropy, to degeneration and change, since he no longer lives in time, but in eternity; he lives outside becoming.

This is why Jesus is as powerful today as he was two thousand years ago when he was living a human life on earth. His "Come, follow me," uttered today in the depths of our hearts, has the same force as when it was said to the apostles. And, to be sure, we see many, many young people forsaking all at the sound of that voice (often much more than the apostles forsook) to follow him.

2. *The hero and the poet: the example of Paul the apostle*

The word of Jesus acts of its own, with an intrinsic force—as St. Paul says, by virtue of just being heard (cf. Rom 10:17). The important thing, he writes to the Philippians, is that Christ be proclaimed, no matter whether in a spirit of rivalry or of good will (cf. Phil 1:15-18). Once sown, whether the farmer sleeps or keeps watch, the seed will grow of its own accord, he knows not how (cf. Mark 4:26f.).

However it must be said that the power contained in the name of Jesus does not normally become active except through the faith of the proclaimer, not through the mere proclamation of the Word. The true Christian proclamation (the *kerygma*) does not consist in conveying propositions about the faith but in conveying the faith itself. Saying, "Jesus is Lord" is saying something about oneself as well; it is the same as saying, "Jesus is *my* Lord!"

It goes without saying, therefore, that an intimate relationship with Jesus, made up of absolute devotion, deep friendship, and admiration, is the secret of the true proclaimer of the gospel. Kierkegaard has a passage of great psychological finesse on the relationship between the hero and the poet or orator, which he uses in his panegyric of Abraham:

> The God who created man and woman also fashioned the hero and the poet or orator. The latter cannot do what the former does; he can only admire, love, rejoice with the hero. All the same, he too is happy, no less than the other. Indeed the hero is his better essence, he with whom he is in love, happy

39

in not being him himself. And this is how his love can manifest itself: in admiration. He is the recording genius who can do nothing save record what has been done, do nothing but admire what has been done, does nothing of himself but is jealous of what has been entrusted to him. He follows his heart's choice but, once having found what he seeks, he then goes from door to door with his songs and his speeches, proclaiming that all should admire the hero as he does, should be as proud of the hero as he is. This is his trade, his humble activity, this is his loyal service in the house of the hero.[1]

We cannot read this passage without thinking of the relationship between St. Paul and Jesus. For Paul, Jesus is the hero; he is in love with him; he is his "better essence." Where Jesus is concerned, Paul would like to disappear so that Jesus may be admired and loved: "We do not preach ourselves but Christ Jesus as Lord!" Elsewhere, significantly, he calls him "Christ Jesus *my* Lord" (cf. Phil 3:8), thus expressing all his humble pride in Jesus, all his love for him. Compared with the supreme good of knowing him, all else henceforth to Paul seems "loss" and "rubbish."

For Paul, Jesus is no mental abstraction, no myth; he is an existing, living person. "To know him . . ." he says (Phil 3:10), and in this pronoun "him" more is said than in whole treatises: him, the Risen One; he who loved me, Jesus "in flesh and bone". . . . Such is his passion for Jesus that he longs to be released from the body solely to "be with Christ," to be able to know him and possess him completely (cf. Phil 1:21f.).

But it is impossible to sound the depths of the relationship between Paul the preacher and Jesus his hero. It is a total dependence. Paul is convinced, and says so, that he has nothing of his own to say, apart from Jesus; nothing new. Everything he says, he takes from him. People go on talking about Paul of Tarsus as the second founder, even, according to some, the true founder of Christianity. But this is an absurdity which would have outraged the Apostle. Paul exists in function of Jesus. Like John the Baptist, he is "the Bridegroom's friend" who rejoices to hear the Bridegroom's voice and retires as soon as he appears. Like the Forerunner, he protests, "I am not the Christ! I am nothing!" What is Paul? he exclaims, addressing the Corinthians: a minister through whom you received the faith; no one can lay a different foundation from the one already there, namely Jesus

Christ (cf. 1 Cor 3:5, 11). As much as to say: there is no room for other founders in the Church; Jesus is the one foundation and the only founder.

Between Paul and Jesus there is a relationship analogous to the one which exists between Jesus and the Father. Jesus, too, protests, saying, "I do not speak on my own account. . . . The words I say to you are not mine but the Father's!" Jesus, too, in a certain sense, is the "recording genius," the admiring genius: he is a poet and his hero is the Father.

A man such as Paul, made incandescent by Jesus as iron by fire, becomes a power for proclaiming. Neither chains nor prisons can stop him; from his captivity come some of his most ardent letters about Jesus, notably the one to the Philippians. How many hearts Paul has inflamed with love for Jesus in these twenty centuries, how many more he will inflame before the end of the world! Of him, Jesus appearing in person to Ananias said, "This man is a chosen instrument of mine to carry my name before Gentiles, kings, and Israelites, and I will show him what he will have to suffer for my name" (Acts 9:15f.). "I shall show him how much he will have to suffer"; I shall show this to him, not to other people; only he and I will know what he has to suffer. It is like this even today for those whom Christ chooses to carry his name before peoples and kings: he who calls us to carry his name calls us also to carry his cross. Only so can the poet share in the inner life and mystery of his hero, and the two claim really to know each other.

3. *"We want to see Jesus"*

"We do not preach ourselves, but Christ Jesus as Lord"; now we are the ones who have to adopt Paul's program ourselves: preaching Jesus as Lord. Satan fears this above all things: not that we should deliver long and learned discourses on every type of problem, but that we should speak about Jesus, that we should proclaim that Jesus is God, that we should preach his victory and the unconquerable power of his blood. (Oh, this is vitriol to his skin, making him react with impressive violence!) Satan goes mad with jealousy about Jesus when he hears someone with faith proclaim that "the wedding day of the Lamb has come; his bride

41

has made herself ready" (Rev 19:7). This then is what we ought to preach in simple terms, with not too many frills: the certainty that "all is accomplished," that the outcome of the long struggle is already decided and there will be no going back to the situation as it was before. In a word, we ought to proclaim that Jesus is "Lord," since everything is contained in this one word.

I remember how impressed I was a few years ago at an interdenominational congress in Kansas City. In the evening we all assembled in the stadium for a time of communal prayer and listening. There were about forty thousand of us, half of whom were Catholics and half of whom belonged to other Christian groups. We prayed in a great spirit of unity, and when one of the brethren invited us, on God's behalf, to repent and bewail the fact "that the body of Christ is divided," in no time the members of this vast crowd sank one by one sobbing to their knees. Above the stadium, against the dark background of the summer sky, stood out a huge sign: "Jesus is Lord." For a moment I seemed to have before my eyes a prophetic image of the unity the Spirit summons us to achieve: one Church reunited by repentance (and possibly by some terrible ordeal) under the lordship of Christ and proclaiming this lordship in the face of heaven and earth.

One may very well say that everything has already been seen to, that there is nothing to be done that hasn't been done already: we talk so much about Jesus, even about Jesus as Lord! Yet this is not the case; there is something missing in us preachers, something concerning the substance, not the externals. We need to rekindle that relationship with Jesus as Lord living in the Spirit, from whom all strength comes. The strength of the risen Jesus is as intact today as it was on the very day when he rose; the "current" of grace has in no respect grown weaker. But we need to put the "plug" of faith into this "socket" so that light-giving contact can be made, and to do this again and again because it has a tendency to keep coming out. Human beings like us cannot sustain a regime of high, supernatural tension; the supernatural is not natural for us! We therefore tend to keep unplugging ourselves, even if unintentionally, adjusting to our own capacity and adjusting the supernatural realities to our capacity too. So, instead of Jesus as Lord living and working in the Spirit, we find ourselves back again working with ideas about Jesus, theories about Jesus, or even dogmas about Jesus. But the dogmas about Jesus are not Jesus, and until we grasp this we have grasped nothing. Dogmas at best are negative definitions of revealed truth; they say what it is not; they are apophatic; they serve to exclude errors about Jesus (at Nicaea the error of Arius, at Ephesus the error ascribed to Nestorius, at Calcedon the error of Eutyches); but we do not say that this is Jesus. Indeed the mystery of the person of the risen Jesus transcends all positive definition; it is attained by faith, an act at once obscure and very bright, which in no way exhausts its object but which nonetheless puts us into true contact with it, as living being with living being. We cannot reach this reality by ways other than those laid out in the dogmas (and it is in this that their perennial value resides), but we cannot reach it if we halt at the dogmas. Human beings are not converted by having truths about Jesus presented to them but by having Jesus himself presented to them. Without realizing what they are doing our contemporaries are asking the Church for what long ago some Greeks asked the apostles: "We want to see Jesus" (cf. John 12:21).

NOTES

1. Søren Kierkegaard, *Fear and Trembling* (Panegyric of Abraham).

Chapter V

"FOR EVERY CARELESS WORD . . ."

Word of God and words of ours

In Matthew's Gospel, in the context of the discourse on words that reveal the heart, a saying of Jesus is recorded that has made readers of the gospel tremble down the ages: "I tell you, on the day of judgement people will render an account for every careless word they speak" (Matt 12:36).

It has always been hard to explain what Jesus meant by "careless word" (*verbum otiosum,* according to the Vulgate). The saying seems divorced from its context, even if the sentence, "You breed of vipers, how can you say good things when you are evil?" (v. 34) already contains a principle of interpretation, apparently meaning that, of their own accord, human beings can only say evil, useless words, themselves being intrinsically evil. A stronger light, however, comes to us from another passage in Matthew's Gospel (7:15-20), where the whole pericope from chapter 12 recurs in almost identical form, and the entire discourse seems to be directed against false prophets: "Beware of false prophets, who come to you in sheep's clothing, but underneath are ravenous wolves. By their fruits you will know them . . ."

If the first-quoted saying of Jesus has some connection with the one about the false prophets, perhaps we shall be able to discover what the word "careless" means. The Greek word is *argòn,* which means "ineffective" (*a,* privative, plus *ergos,* "work"). Modern translations render it as "unfounded," hence with a passive sense: a word which is groundless, hence a calumny. But this seems to be an attempt to give a more reassuring meaning to Jesus' terrible threat. There is nothing particularly alarming in Jesus' saying every calumny will have to be accounted for to God! But the meaning of *argòn* is more properly active: a word that "founds" nothing, produces nothing, hence which is empty, sterile. In this sense the Vulgate translation was more correct: an "otiose," useless word.

It will not be hard to guess what Jesus has in mind if we compare this adjective with the one in the Bible that constantly characterizes the Word of God: the adjective *energes*, "efficacious," that which works, which always produces a result (*ergos*)—the same adjective from which the word *energetic* is derived. St. Paul, for instance, writes to the Thessalonians that they, on receiving the divine word of the Apostle's teaching, have heard it not as human words but as it truly is, as "the Word of God which is at work [*energeitai*] in those who believe" (cf. 1 Thess 2:13). The difference between the Word of God and human words is here presented, implicitly, as the difference between the Word that works and the word that does not work, between the efficacious Word and the inefficacious, empty word. So, too, in the Epistle to the Hebrews we find this concept of the efficacity of the divine Word: "The Word of God is living and effective [*energes*]" (Heb 4:12). But this is a concept of ancient pedigree. In Isaiah, God declares that the word issuing from his mouth will never return to him "without effect," without having achieved the end for which he sent it out (cf. Isa 55:11).

The useless word, which human beings will have to account for on Judgement Day, is not, therefore, any old useless word; it is the useless, empty word uttered by people who ought instead to be uttering the "energetic" words of God and at the time when they ought to be uttering them. It is, in a word, the word of the false prophet, who draws the word out of his own evil heart, who can only produce useless words, who does not receive the word from God yet induces other people to believe it is the word of God. What happens is precisely the opposite of what St. Paul was saying: having received a human word, they take it not for what it is but for what it is not, namely, a divine word. For every useless word about God we shall have to render an account! This, then, is the meaning of Jesus' grave warning.

The useless word is the counterfeit, the parasite of the Word of God. It can be recognized by the fruits that it does not produce, since, by definition, it is sterile, inefficacious. God "watches over his word" (cf. Jer 1:12), he is jealous of it and will not

45

allow human beings to usurp the divine power contained in it; he is terrible against this sin of the false prophets.

As through an amplifier, the prophet Jeremiah lets us hear the cry concealed behind this saying of Jesus'. Let us listen. (Here it is made quite clear that he has in mind the false prophets.)

Thus says the LORD of hosts:

"Listen not to the words of your prophets,
    who fill you with emptiness;
Visions of their own fancy they speak,
    not from the mouth of the LORD. . . .

Let the prophet who has a dream recount his dream [i.e., say openly that it is one of his own dreams]; let him who has my word speak my word truthfully!

What has straw to do with the wheat?
    says the LORD.
Is not my word like fire, says the LORD,
    like a hammer shattering rocks?

Therefore I am against the prophets, says the LORD, who steal my words from each other" (Jer 23:16, 28-30).

1. Who the false prophets are

What do straw and wheat have in common, or straw and fire? What does the dream have in common with reality? What, says God, do your words have in common with my word? So why are you so often tempted to substitute one for the other?

But we are not giving a lecture on false prophets in the Bible. We are trying to capture God's complaint against the false prophets and apply it to ourselves and our own times. For, as ever, it is of us the Bible is speaking and to us it speaks. Jesus' saying is not a judgement on the world but on the Church; the world will not be judged over useless words (all its words, in the sense described above, are useless ones!) but, at most, for not having believed in Jesus (cf. John 16:9). The people who will have to render an account for every useless word are the preachers of the Word of God. Who does not tremble at this point? I do.

The false prophets are not just those who from time to time spread heresies (as people usually suppose) but are also those who

46

"falsify" the Word of God. Paul uses this term, taking it from the language of the day; literally it means watering down the Word, like fraudulent innkeepers putting water in their wine (cf. 2 Cor 2:17; 4:2). The false prophets are those who do not present the Word of God in its purity but dilute it and weaken it in the thousands of human words issuing from their own hearts. The false prophet, alas! is me every time (and it happens often) I do not rely on the "weakness," "foolishness," poverty, and nakedness of the Word but try to dress it up and attach more importance to the dress than to the Word, spending more time on the dressing than in standing in prayer before the Word itself, in worshipping it and in getting it to start living in me. At Cana in Galilee, Jesus turned the water into wine, that is to say the dead letter into the life-giving Spirit (for such was the spiritual interpretation that the Fathers put on his action); the false prophets are those who do the very opposite, who turn the pure wine of the Word of God into water which cannot inebriate anyone, that is, into dead letter and idle chatter. Deep down, they are ashamed of the gospel (cf. Rom 1:16) and the words of Jesus as being too hard for the world, or too poor and naked for the learned, and so they try to spice them up with what Jeremiah called "visions of their own fancy." St. Paul, writing to his disciple Timothy, said, "Be eager to present yourself as acceptable to God, a workman . . . imparting the word of truth without deviation. Avoid profane, idle talk, for such people will become more and more godless" (2 Tim 2:15-16).

God is provoked by the profane, idle chatter that goes on in his Church. ("Profane" means having no connection with God's plan, having nothing to do with the Church's mission.) Too many human words, too many useless words, too many speeches, too many papers. The gospel saying has come true: the children ask for bread, but instead they are given stones (cf. Matt 7:9), dead words which cannot satisfy hunger, words that do not taste of God. In the age of mass communication the Church is in danger, at least in affluent countries, of burrowing into the straw of useless words, of talking for the sake of talking, of writing because the reviews and magazines are there to be filled. It is a new Noah's Flood, from which few souls are saved today too. How can the world perceive the energetic Word of God in the hubbub of useless words emanating from the Church? We offer the world the

47

best of excuses for sitting tight in its unbelief and its sins. If unbelievers could so much as hear the authentic Word of God, they would not find it so easy to get away with saying (as they often do after hearing our sermons): "Words, words, words!" The human race and the Church, too, are sick with uproar; we need "to declare a fast" from words. We need someone to shout, as Moses once did: "Be silent, O Israel, and listen!" (Deut 27:9).

2. "Jesus did not come to tell us fairy-tales"

These words of Péguy's have always stuck in my mind. As before, the Church is addressing her children. She says:

Jesus Christ, my girl,
did not come to tell us fairy-tales. . . .
He did not make the journey down to earth
to come and ask us riddles and crack jokes.
He had not got the time to lark about. . . .
He did not expend his life . . .
in coming to tell us nonsense stories.[1]

Jesus for his part never said useless words. His words were all "Spirit and life" (cf. John 6:63). He did not try to get himself accepted by means of charming talk, putting other people at their ease and cutting a fine figure himself. He simply offered "the words of God" (John 3:34), and with these few and unadorned words he changed the face of the earth. He did not invent anything himself; he just said the words the Father had commanded him to say (cf. John 12:49).

In the New Testament we find precise directions for finding out just what, in this sphere, is the object of God's anger. In Mark's Gospel, Jesus quotes the words of Isaiah: "In vain do they worship me, teaching as doctrine human precepts" (Mark 7:7). Then he goes on, addressing the Pharisees and scribes: "You disregard God's commandment but cling to human tradition. . . . You nullify the Word of God in favor of your tradition that you have handed on" (Mark 7:7-13). When we cannot manage to set forth the plain and naked Word of God without passing it through the oily filter of this or that ecclesiastical tradition (not the Tradition we talked about earlier)—traditions made up of thousands of distinctions and clarifications and additions and explanations, in themselves absolutely fine but which dilute the Word of God— we are doing exactly what Jesus reproached the Pharisees and scribes for doing in their day: "nullifying" the Word of God; "trapping it in a net"; making it lose the greater part of its strength to penetrate the human heart.

Another example of what Scripture means when condemning "useless" words is to be found at the beginning of the First Epistle to the Corinthians, where the Apostle attacks those who seek to dissolve the *kerygma* of the Cross into human wisdom in such a way as to make it acceptable, not because it comes from God, period, but mainly so that the human mind will find that this corresponds to what it normally regards as worthy of attention, since it can fit into a given view of the world. Against the "word of the Cross," every human word is "useless" and should fall silent, cries the Apostle, unless one wishes to render the word of the Cross "useless" (emptied) as well. To clothe the *kerygma* of the Cross in words of human wisdom (and human vanity) is to commit the same outrage the soldiers committed when they put a purple mantle on the back of the scourged and naked Jesus, and a sham scepter in his hand.

The Word of God revolts against being reduced to ideology. Ideology is what is left once the current from the Word of God has been cut off, once the word has been unplugged from the transcendent and personal reality of God, so that it is no longer the Word disposing of me and leading me where it chooses but I who am disposing of it and leading it where I choose. God will not tolerate his almighty Word being used to garnish a speech for this occasion or that, nor to cloak with divine authority speeches already composed and entirely human. In recent times we have seen where such a tendency can lead. The gospel has been exploited in support of every kind of human project, from class war to the death of God. But this is all old hat. At the beginning of our century there appeared a history of interpretations of the life of Jesus which conclusively demonstrated that, in all historical and critical research from the Age of Enlightenment onwards, the gospel has been bent this way and that to say whatever happened to be socially fashionable at any given period. Thus the Word of God has been used to endorse human projects, when, contrariwise, everything should be endorsing the Word of God.

When the reactions of an audience are so predetermined by psychological, trade-unionist, political, or emotional conditioning as initially to make it impossible for the preacher not to say what the audience is expecting to hear and not admit that it is completely right; when there is no hope of one's being able to bring one's listeners round to the point when one can say, "Repent and believe!", the fact is that it is preferable not to proclaim the Word of God than to have it subordinated to party interests and so betrayed. It is better to abandon the idea of making a true and proper proclamation and to confine oneself at most to listening, trying to understand and share the anxieties and sufferings of these people, and to preach the gospel of the kingdom by one's presence and charity instead.

The facts of experience and, hence, the human word, are obviously not to be excluded from the Church's preaching, but they must be entirely subject to the Word of God and at its service. As in the Eucharist it is the Body of Christ that assimilates to itself whoever eats it, and not the other way round, so, in preaching the gospel, the Word of God has to be the dominant living principle, subjecting and assimilating the human word to itself, not vice-versa. When dealing with the Church's doctrinal and disciplinary problems, therefore, we need bravely to start out more often from the Word of God, especially as revealed in the New Testament, and stay bound to it, chained to it, certain that in this way we shall much more surely achieve our purpose, which is, in any question, to discover where the will of God lies.

Speaking of Israel's deliverance from Egypt, the Book of Wisdom says, "Neither herb nor poultice cured them, but your all-healing Word, O Lord!" (cf. Wis 16:12). Similarly, the ills of Christians will not be cured by applying poultices (i.e., human remedies) but by the living, all-healing Word of God.

3. *Preaching with the words of God*

Never has Scripture been read and studied as much as today; never has it been talked about as much as today. Yet I feel we should take Christ's severe warning about "useless" words very much to heart, particularly today, since never before has the mass of human verbiage been so dense as to threaten to suffocate the Word of God. The Word of God is under threat from verbal inflation.

Speaking of the childhood of Samuel, Scripture says, "The word of the Lord was rare in those days" (cf. 1 Sam 3:1). Did people in Israel talk much about God in the days of Samuel? Certainly, but nonetheless, "the word of God was rare." For the Word of God is different from our talking about God; it is God who does the talking and we who do the listening! Despite all the talking we do today about God and the Bible, I can't help wondering whether someone setting out tomorrow to write the spiritual history of our times ought not also to begin by saying, "The Word of God was rare in those days!"

What is needed is obviously not just biblical quotations, however fine and pregnant they may be, but prophetic words, words emerging from much suffering and much prayer, which can bring the hearer face to face with the actual presence and lordship of the risen Christ. We have all experienced how much one single Word of God can do, if deeply believed and lived by the person who proclaims it, even if sometimes unawares; priests often experience that among all their countless words there is one that goes to the heart and leads more than one person who hears it to the confessional. Indeed there are no words like this word. In the prophet Isaiah there is an obscure passage that used to be translated as follows: "God gave the law so that they might say, 'There is nothing like this word'" (cf. Isa 8:20). Commenting on this verse, Origen says, "There are words, but they are not like that one. For after the word of Moses, after the word of the prophets and again after the words of Jesus Christ and his apostles, there is no further word. With all the more reason can the Church exclaim today: 'There is no word like this word . . .' No, there is no word to be compared with the one which the Church has received and by which she is saved."[2]

This is why the Apostle Peter very wisely exhorts us when he says, "Whoever preaches, let it be with the words of God" (1 Pet 4:11). Not always, indeed hardly ever, can we know for sure whether God is really speaking through us, whether a given word that we proclaim comes from God's heart or our own, whether it is an "efficacious" or a "useless" one. For we are indeed dealing with something imperceptible and mysterious, as is every "passing-by" of the Lord's; it is a kind of interference that intrudes into the preacher's voice at a certain moment without his being aware of it, but which the listener, touched by grace, perceives sometimes, as it were, with a shiver.

We cannot know, as I have said, when God is speaking, in the strongest sense of the expression; but we for our part can at least create the right conditions for him to do so. St. Paul seems to be summing up these conditions when he writes, "We are not like the many who trade on [lit. water down, falsify] the Word of God; but as out of sincerity, indeed as from God and in the presence of God, we speak in Christ" (2 Cor 2:17). The favorable conditions, therefore, are to speak in Christ sincerely as though moved by God, not by other interests: to speak under his gaze. The preacher who strives to speak under God's gaze is preserved from the plague of vainglory (when God makes his voice heard "the earth fears and falls silent," says the psalmist [cf. Ps 76:9]; when "the lion roars" human beings tremble, says Amos) and he is also preserved from saying too many "useless" words. In proportion to the hidden contact between our hearts and God's heart and gaze, the living Word of God will issue from our mouths to edify the faithful.

In that same passage the Apostle asked himself, "Who is qualified for this?" (2 Cor 2:16). No one is qualified for this. "We hold this treasure in earthen vessels" (2 Cor 4:7). We can only say, Lord, have pity on this poor earthen vessel which has to hold the treasure of your Word; preserve us from useless words; let us once experience the taste of your Word so that in the future we can distinguish it from any other, and so that any other may seem insipid to us. Pour into the midst of your people, as you have promised, hunger and thirst for your Word; "fill Zion—the Church—with your majesty, and your people with your glory . . . and let your prophets be proved true" (cf. Sir 36:13, 15).

NOTES

1. Ch. Péguy, "Le porche du mystère de la deuxième vertu," 585–86.
2. Origen, *Homilia in Isaiam* 7.4 (GCS, 1925, p. 285).

Chapter VI

"YOU WILL RECEIVE POWER FROM THE HOLY SPIRIT"

The Holy Spirit and the proclamation of the Word

Let us begin this meditation by listening, before anything else, to a word of Jesus', indeed the last he spoke on earth before he ascended into heaven. When the apostles asked him if the time had finally come for him to restore the sovereignty of Israel, Jesus replied, "It is not for you to know the times or seasons that the Father has established by his own authority. But you will receive power when the holy Spirit comes upon you, and you will be my witnesses in Jerusalem, throughout Judea and Samaria, and to the ends of the earth" (Acts 1:7-8).

In the language of the New Testament, the expressions "witnessing to Jesus" and "bearing witness" correspond exactly to what we today mean by the words *evangelization* and *evangelize*. These words of Jesus are therefore saying something very important: the Holy Spirit is the power of evangelization and the very condition of its being possible. We are constantly holding meetings and carrying out studies on the topic of evangelization; in them we mainly study the forms, means, techniques, and problems of evangelization, and new demands such as the promotion of human values, inculturation, and the signs of the times. Here and now, however, we shall not concentrate so much on the forms but rather on the inner reality of evangelization: its soul. Years ago, when we were being trained, there was a book we all found helpful; it was originally written in French by Abbé Chautard and its title was *The Soul of Every Apostolate*. Nowadays what was then called "soul" has recovered its proper name; it is called the Holy Spirit! The soul of any Christian proclamation is not a thing, not even a vastly important thing like prayer, but a person; it is the same Person who is the soul of the Church.

The fundamental rule of Christian proclamation is: "To preach Christ in the Holy Spirit" or, as we find in a passage in the First Epistle of Peter: "To preach the gospel in the Holy Spirit" (cf. 1 Pet 1:12). "Christ" or "the gospel" indicates the *content* of the preaching; "in the Holy Spirit" indicates the *method,* the way in which the preaching has to be done. In the two previous meditations I spoke about the content of Christian preaching, showing that this consists in God's efficacious words and, most particularly, in the Word which sums up and perpetuates all God's words to the human race: "Christ Jesus is Lord." It therefore remains for us to speak of the method, that is, of the Holy Spirit.

1. *"The Spirit of the Lord is upon me"*

We must go back to the first evangelizer, Jesus of Nazareth. St. Luke tells us that, immediately after overcoming the temptation in the wilderness, "Jesus returned to Galilee in the power of the Spirit and . . . taught in their synagogues" (Luke 4:14f.). All Jesus' evangelistic activity, beginning at this moment, is thus placed under the action of the Holy Spirit. Jesus himself, in any case, declares as much in his address in the synagogue at Nazareth, when he says, "The Spirit of the Lord is upon me . . . he has anointed me to bring glad tidings to the poor" (Luke 4:18).

The Spirit is thus conferred on Jesus primarily for the purpose of bringing the glad tidings, for evangelization. He does not give Jesus the word to be proclaimed (for Jesus is himself the Word made flesh), but gives power to his word; thus, he is the very power of Jesus' word. The Holy Spirit makes the word of Jesus an "efficacious" word; when Jesus speaks, wonders always follow: the paralyzed man stands up, the sea grows calm, the fig tree dries out, the blind recover their sight.

Speaking of the Messiah, Isaiah says, "He shall strike the ruthless with the rod of his mouth/and with the breath of his lips he shall slay the wicked" (Isa 11:4). And just so, when Jesus speaks, Satan is struck and falls like a thunderbolt from the sky; the demons are as though "scorched" by his words and come out shouting, "You have come to destroy us!" Such is the extraordinary power operating in this Word.

Above all, the Spirit gives Jesus the strength not to become dejected (cf. Isa 42:3); he strengthens him more with a view to failure than to success, in as much as the former is implicit in his mission as Suffering Servant. Constancy, generosity, strength, unction, wisdom, piety: all the gifts of the Spirit, set out in the famous passage in Isaiah (11:1ff.), and an infinite number of other ones as well, shine in the evangelistic activity of the Messiah, and it is natural that this should be so, if it is true that from him flow every grace and every spiritual gift. The Spirit of the Lord hence impels Jesus to evangelize: not only as an outside force, but actually following him and helping him in the unfolding of his mission, making himself, as St. Basil says, "his inseparable companion."[1]

If now, from Jesus, we pass to the Church, we observe the identical relationship with the Holy Spirit; what happened in the Head is repeated in the body. If the Church had had a voice, after Pentecost she would, like Jesus, have been able to exclaim, "The Spirit of the Lord is upon me, he has anointed me to bring glad tidings to the poor!" The entire Acts of the Apostles is summed up in this exclamation. Having received the Holy Spirit, Peter, with the other Eleven, sets out through the streets of Jerusalem to preach Christ crucified, and his word has so mysterious a power that people on hearing him speak, feel "cut to the heart," are "convinced of sin" by the Holy Spirit, and exclaim, "What are we to do, my brothers?" (Acts 2:37).

During his life on earth, Jesus had predicted that the Holy Spirit would give his apostles an "irresistible" word (cf. Luke 21:15; Matt 10:20; Mark 13:11) and in fact when Stephen speaks about Jesus before the Sanhedrin, we read that his adversaries "could not withstand the wisdom and the spirit with which he spoke" (Acts 6:10). It is moving to see all Christ's promises concerning the Holy Spirit coming true, one after another, after Pentecost. He had for instance said, "When the Advocate comes . . . he will testify to me and you too will testify" (cf. John 15:26f.), and now we hear Peter in Acts exclaiming as he addresses the crowds after speaking about Jesus, "We are witnesses of these things, as is the holy Spirit that God has given to those who obey him" (Acts 5:32). Thus, from the outset, evangelization can be seen as the result of two conjoint testimonies: the human and visible testimony of the apostles and, subsequently, of the Church, and the invisible and divine testimony of the Spirit acting behind it.

The testimony of the Spirit is of course invisible in itself but makes itself visible and as it were palpable in the effects it produces and the signs that accompany it. St. Paul says, "My message and my proclamation were not with persuasive words of wisdom, but with a demonstration of the Spirit and his power" (cf. 1 Cor 2:4). Thus in evangelization we can distinguish two types of manifestation of the Spirit: the first is given in "signs, wonders, and miracles" (cf. 2 Cor 12:12) which accompany the preaching and are directed primarily at the listeners so that they may believe; the other is given in the charisms which, by contrast, are destined straight for the preacher, so that he may be equal to his task. Among those charisms particularly associated with evangelization, the Apostle often mentions the gifts of eloquence, wisdom, knowledge, teaching, and prophecy. All these things are defined as "particular manifestations of the Spirit for the common use" (cf. 1 Cor 12:7). Therefore they make the Spirit manifest and visible!

The texts quoted above are enough to let us grasp how the primitive Christian community regarded the Holy Spirit as the great driving force of the Word, guiding its race, in breadth, to the very ends of the earth and, in depth, into the innermost hearts of the faithful. Between the Word and the Spirit there exists the same relationship as that between the sword and the person who wields it. The Word of God is a double-edged sword "penetrating even between soul and spirit . . . and able to discern reflections and thoughts of the heart" (Heb 4:12); but this sword, St. Paul makes clear, is "the sword of the Spirit" (Eph 6:17), the instrument the Holy Spirit employs to change people's hearts. An evangelization without the quickening breath of the Holy Spirit is like a sharp sword which is left aside and never brandished. It will not "cut to the heart."

So the Spirit gives strength and vigor not only to the word proclaimed but also to the proclaimer. St. Ambrose, commenting on the verse in the Psalms that says, "The flood has raised up its roar . . ." (Ps 93:3), wrote to a fellow-bishop:

> There are rivers that flow from the belly of him who drinks from Christ and partakes of the Spirit of God. These rivers therefore when they redound with the grace of the Spirit, lift up their voice. There is also a stream which overflows upon his holy ones like a torrent. . . . Whoever receives of the fullness of this stream, like John the Evangelist, like Peter and Paul,

lifts up his voice. Just as the apostles with the harmony of their message spread the sound of their preaching of the gospel to all the ends of the earth, so also does he begin to tell the good tidings of the Lord Jesus. Drink, then, from Christ so that your sound, too, may go out.[2]

2. *The silence of the Spirit*

We shall now jump from apostolic times to our own. If we look at the state of Christian proclamation, at least in modern (i.e., post-Reformation) Europe, we note one dominant characteristic. This is first to be found at the highest levels of philosophical and theological speculation, but then, as is always the case, it tends to spread out and to some degree condition all Christian proclamation. St. Paul said he had deliberately never attempted to base his preaching on "persuasive words of wisdom," lest the faith of his listeners should be founded on human wisdom, but only on the power of God (cf. 1 Cor 2:5). Precisely what the Apostle was afraid of has come about among ourselves; preaching becomes ever more remote from "the power of the Spirit," appealing to "human wisdom," even though a wisdom theological in type. The difference is immense. Addresses based on human wisdom are by nature persuasive and persuade their listeners (if they persuade them of anything) to give a purely human and intellectual assent, whereas Christian preaching, though it is a demonstration (as we have said, it manifests the power of the Spirit), claims assent of a different order: the order of the Spirit, not of the flesh or of the letter. The flesh indeed, as Jesus said, "is of no avail" (cf. John 6:63); it avails to make scholars but not to make "justified" Christians.

Not wishing to generalize too much and well aware that there have been splendid exceptions, we might say that as far as Christian preaching is concerned, we in the West have witnessed a massive relapse into the letter and the flesh. The prevailing rationalism requires Christianity to present its message in dialectical form, that is, subjecting every aspect of it to discussion and research, so that it can fit into the general, philosophically acceptable picture of an effort on the part of human nature to understand itself and the universe (H. Schlier). And so the saving proclamation about the dead and risen Christ has been subjected to another purpose and ceased to try to subdue all things to itself (as is in its nature).

Kierkegaard effectively denounced the presumptuousness of much of modern thought in trying to go beyond faith (as if there were anything beyond faith!), contrasting this attitude with that of Abraham, who was content simply to believe. This presumptuousness is still at work in that part of contemporary thought where research, and not the truth, is the absolute; where God is accepted, on condition that he ever be a God who is researched but never found, and Christ is accepted too, on condition that he be one of the revealers of God but not himself the definitive revelation of God. The absolute, it is said, kills research (Jaspers), kills conscience (Merleau-Ponty); the absolute, in short, kills humanity (Sartre).

The actual problem is more deeply hidden. Why are modern people afraid of certainty? Why instead of the truth do they hold the search for truth as the supreme good? Simply because, as long as the research phase lasts, the human individual and thinker is the protagonist who determines values and morality, whereas, faced with the truth recognized as such, we have no way out left and have to obey. Obedience is the real hub of the problem; at the bottom of everything there is always the age-old temptation to be "like God." "It is true that the absolute kills humanity," but only humanity as seduced by the serpent, but not true humanity.

Now, St. Paul says that "to break down fortresses, destroy arguments and every pretension raising itself against the knowledge of God and to take every thought captive in obedience to Christ," weapons "of flesh" are not sufficient; spiritual ones are needed. So reason and human wisdom are not enough; we need "the power of the Spirit" (cf. 2 Cor 10:3-5; Rom 15:18-19). In other words, reason cannot subdue reason and reduce it to "the obedience of faith" (Rom 1:5), but this can be done by something standing above reason, which is divine truth (which, however, acts through reason, not contrary to it: not destroying it but saving it).

Unfortunately, we must admit that Christian proclaimers have often let themselves become too much conditioned by what "the world" requires and have responded with an ever "wiser," historically and speculatively based preaching, and which is by the same token ever less kerygmatic (i.e., based on the indisputable au-

58

thority of God). We are in a sense direct heirs of those Greeks who, according to Paul, sought wisdom and regarded the preaching of Christ crucified as foolishness (cf. 1 Cor 1:23).

Parallel with this, we note that the *idea* has taken precedence over reality and over *life*. Idealism is the acute form of this malady but not the only one; all Western culture and theology these days, especially in Northern Europe, are fundamentally ideological. Thus the living God is reduced to "the idea of the living God" (which is something quite different!); similarly, the Holy Spirit, for Hegel, is an idea, the idea of the Absolute Spirit.

In environments that have remained more closely bound to the Catholic Church, idealism and rationalism, as doctrine, have less of a hold, but this is no reason for claiming that these places more clearly manifest the Spirit and its power. Here the evil is legalism and juridicism, which are another way of relapsing into the letter and the flesh.

We might compare (with all due reservations) the last two or three centuries in Europe—those characterised by the Enlightenment—with the two or three centuries preceding the coming of Christ in Israel, known as the centuries of "the silence of the Spirit and of prophecy." Not, of course, that the Spirit had forsaken the Church (if that had happened the Church would have ceased to exist), but his activity was certainly slowed down and as it were hidden under a blanket of forgetfulness and lack of interest.

3. *A new Pentecost*

If we now turn our attention to the Church of our own day, with amazement and joy we recognize new factors which profoundly modify this state of "silence of the Spirit." With our human limitations, we can only seize on a few elements of this grandiose work of the Spirit in our age, and perhaps not the profoundest, those occurring deep within souls and only manifest many years later. But even those few elements that we are able to seize on are enough to fill us with gratitude and hope.

Undoubtedly the most important thing of all has been the Second Vatican Council. In summoning it, Pope John XXIII was inspired with the boldness to pray to God for "a new Pentecost" for the Church; and the risen Lord, who hears the prayers addressed to him by his vicar on earth at crucial times in the Church's

59

life, answered that prayer. The Holy Spirit, having been the inspirer, has revealed himself ever more clearly with the passing of the years as the true accomplisher of the council. In his letter for the sixteenth centenary of the Ecumenical Council of Constantinople, John Paul II wrote: "None of *the work of renewal in the Church* which the Second Vatican Council has thus providentially proposed and initiated . . . can be accomplished except *in the Holy Spirit,* that is to say with the help of his light and his power."[3] In his closing address to the Pneumatological Congress, held to commemorate the same event, the Holy Father then clinched the matter, saying, "The Holy Spirit is the source and motor of renewal in Christ's Church."

Previously, Pope Paul VI, in his apostolic exhortation *Evangelii nuntiandi,* had emphasized the role of the Holy Spirit in the work of evangelization:

> It must be said that the Holy Spirit is the principal agent of evangelization: it is he who impels each individual to proclaim the gospel and it is he who in the depths of consciences causes the word of salvation to be accepted and understood. But it can equally be said that he is the goal of evangelization: he alone stirs up the new creation, the new humanity of which evangelization is to be the result, with that unity in variety which evangelization wishes to achieve within the Christian community. Through the Holy Spirit the gospel penetrates to the heart of the world, for it is he who causes people to discern the signs of the times. . . . The Synod of Bishops of 1974, which insisted strongly on the place of the Holy Spirit in evangelization, also expressed the desire that pastors and theologians—and we would also say the faithful marked by the seal of the Spirit by baptism—should study more thoroughly the nature and manner of the Holy Spirit's action in evangelization today. This is our desire too, and we exhort all evangelizers, whoever they may be, to pray without ceasing to the Holy Spirit with faith and fervor and to let themselves prudently be guided by him as the decisive inspirer of their plans, their initiatives and their evangelizing activity.[4]

4. *The means: obedience, prayer, community*

The Nicene-Constantinopolitan Creed defines the Holy Spirit as "the Lord and giver of life." And here, too, in the sphere of evangelization, this is the fundamental characteristic of his activity. He not only prompts the Church to renew the content and invent new forms of evangelization, but he is also at work "giving life" to all the content and all the forms, be they old or new, whether the lowliest (the contact between person and person) or those more solemn and public (e.g., as preaching, the defence of the faith, and the very teaching of the magisterium).

To obtain this life, however, it is not enough to talk a great deal about the Holy Spirit; there is in fact a danger of creating an ideology even by talking about him. This occurs when we treat him as an idea or a theme, which we scatter here and there in our addresses as one would sugar on a pudding, and not, as we should, as the invisible force permeating all from within.

The practical problem, to which we must now turn our attention, lies precisely here: How are we to let the Spirit act in all we do? How are we to conduct an evangelization which will be truly spiritual? I shall develop three points which strike me as being important to our purpose (even though they are certainly not the only ones) and which I can sum up in three words: obedience, prayer, and community.

Obedience. By the term *obedience* I mean a complex of attitudes which allow us to resemble Jesus. Jesus received the fullness of the Spirit in the Jordan from the Father because in filial obedience he accepted the mission of the suffering and humiliated Messiah, the mission of the Servant, which the Father at that moment had fully revealed to him. "God," says the Apostle Peter, "gives the Holy Spirit to those who obey him" (cf. Acts 5:32).

There must be a dying to self, an allowing of one's heart to be wounded, so as to accept in full the Father's will, which is so utterly great and different from ours. There were many Gethsemane nights in Jesus' life, not merely one; in them he strove with God, but not to bend God to his will (which basically was what Jacob did when he too strove with God) but to bend his own human will to God's and say, at every new difficulty and demand, "Fiat!" After many such nights, he would preach again to the crowds and the crowds, smitten with amazement, would say, "He speaks with authority, doesn't he! Where does he get this authority from?" He certainly spoke with authority. Indeed, he spoke with the authority of God himself, for when one surrenders oneself

61

completely to God, then, mysteriously, God surrenders himself and entrusts one with his Spirit and his power, which he now knows will not be abused for one's own purposes and glory. Then it happens that the words one utters will "cut to the heart."

The power of the Spirit in the proclaimer is proportionate to the harshness of the cross that individual carries. I have already mentioned that the Bible, speaking of the Word of God, often uses the image of the scroll that has to be swallowed, the scroll that is sweet as honey on the lips but bitter as wormwood in the stomach. The Word of God is sweet for others, for those who hear it, but it is bitter for the proclaimer; so, the sweeter and more persuasive it is for others, the bitterer it has been, the more suffering it has involved, for the latter. It is bitter because the Word is a sword which first strikes and cuts the preacher's own sinfulness, exposing inconsistency and hypocrisy; bitter, moreover, because it unites the preacher to the mystery of him who was crucified for the Word's sake.

Prayer. The Spirit comes from the heart of Christ pierced on the cross. We need to be united to that heart in order to receive him, and what keeps us united to that heart is prayer. The Holy Spirit came upon Jesus in the Jordan while he was at prayer (cf. Luke 3:21) and upon the apostles while they "devoted themselves with one accord to prayer" (Acts 1:14). Jesus says the Father gives the Holy Spirit "to those who ask him" (Luke 11:13).

Thanks to prayer, we become—as, at a different level, was Christ's human nature—"conjoint instruments": conjoint, that is, to the Godhead. The word proclaimed is then a living word, as that water is living which gushes straight from the spring, and is not poured from bottles.

Prophecy is a very important gift for the evangelizer. The Book of Revelation says without qualification, "Witness to Jesus is the spirit of prophecy" (Rev 19:10), as much as to say: the soul of evangelization ("witness to Jesus" means evangelization!) is prophecy. Now, the charism of prophecy, when spoken of with reference to evangelization, consists in the ability to convey, as though from the living source, God's judgement or present will to the listener; it consists in putting the listener into the presence of God, *coram Deo,* and sometimes making bold to say, "thus says the Lord." When we speak with this spirit of prophecy, St.

Paul says, and it happens that there are non-believers present, they will feel themselves to be under God's judgement, the secrets of their hearts will be laid bare, and they will not be able to help exclaiming: "God is truly in your midst!" (cf. 1 Cor 14:24f.). For this speaking in the spirit of prophecy to be possible, we have, as it were, to annul ourselves, to make ourselves empty and disposable for God. We are not engaged in the spirit of prophecy in this sense if we first sit down at our desk and choose our topic or what we mean to say, drawing on our own insights or our own culture, and then for good measure get down on our knees and pray God to give life to our words and endue them with his own authority. What we ought to do is the very opposite. First of all, in prayer and on our knees, we should ask God to reveal to us the word he has selected and stored in his heart for a particular situation and people, and after this, at our desk, we should put all our culture and experience at the service of this word.

Community. A third point that I regard as most important is living contact with a praying community, in which the gifts of the Spirit, received in baptism, are lived and exercised. I have often observed how the Word and the power of the Spirit are more willingly given by God to a community at prayer than to an individual. God, it might be said, loves collegiality, because this safeguards humility. We find a significant example of this in the Acts of the Apostles. After the healing of the cripple, Peter and John are led before the Sanhedrin, questioned, and then sent away with the strict order not to preach any more in the name of Jesus. On regaining their freedom, the apostles go to the brethren and tell them what has happened. The situation was critical and has often recurred in the course of the centuries. What was to be done? Go on preaching as before and risk provoking a brutal reaction on the part of the authorities, which might finish everything forever, or keep quiet and so risk betraying Christ's mandate? On their own, the two apostles cannot resolve the dilemma; but now the community falls to prayer and powerful charisms are manifested in their midst. One member reads a passage from Scripture ("Why did the Gentiles rage . . ."); another with prophetic insight applies this text to the present moment ("Indeed they gathered in this city against your holy servant Jesus whom you anointed—Herod and Pontius Pilate together with the Gentiles!");

instantly the situation is illuminated by the Word of God and under its control. This generates the gift of charismatic faith, thanks to which the community makes bold to ask God to work "healings and signs and wonders in the name of Jesus," knowing that God will do so. "As they prayed," the account goes on, "the place where they were gathered shook and they were all filled with the Holy Spirit and went on boldly proclaiming the word of God" (cf. Acts 4:18-31). "Boldly": here again we find the well-known term *parrhesia,* which means free speaking, apostolic boldness. And so it was the community at prayer, with its many charisms, that made it possible for the Christian proclamation to pursue its victorious race.

I think it is a great blessing for proclaimers of the Word and pastors to have access to communities with whom they can pray in that unique humility brought about when Jesus makes himself present in the midst of "two or three gathered together in his name," and when by his mere presence he reduces human and ministerial differences to due proportion, causing all to humble themselves "under the mighty hand of God." In the upper room, the apostles, Mary, and holy women are mentioned together without apparent distinction of status; it is when they come out of the upper room, each to their individual ministry, that their diverse callings become clear and Peter stands apart, together with the other Eleven, while Mary and the women remain in the upper room, silent and hidden.

All together we thank Jesus for showing that he wills, in our own day, through us, once more to fulfill his promise: "You will receive power when the Holy Spirit comes upon you, and you will be my witnesses in Jerusalem, throughout Judea and Samaria and to the ends of the earth."

NOTES

1. St. Basil, *De Spiritu Sancto* 16 (PG 32, 140).
2. St. Ambrose, *Epistula* 2.2 [36.2] (PL 16, 917f.).
3. In *Acta Apostolicae Sedis* 73 (1981), p. 521.
4. Paul VI, *Evangelii nuntiandi* 75.

Chapter VII

"WELCOME THE WORD"

The Word of God in the personal life of the Christian

I began this series of meditations by first of all sketching a picture of the Word in salvation-history; I then spoke of the Word of God in the life of the Church, devoting the central meditations to the theme of the proclamation of the Word. I should now like to devote the final two meditations to a third aspect, or sphere of activity, of the Word: the Word of God in the personal life of the Christian. There are three fundamental levels of the Word of God which, taken together, form the Christian mystery: the historical level, the sacramental level, and the moral level. We have already, at the start, contemplated the Word-event, the Word coming down in time, at precise moments in salvation-history (in Isaiah, in Ezekiel, in John the Baptist) and finally incarnate in Jesus of Nazareth; we next considered the Word-sacrament, the Word as it continues to act in the Church today, through the sign of the divinely inspired Scriptures; now we consider the Word as moral and spiritual principle and guide for the individual believer.

Let us read a famous passage about the Word of God in the Epistle of St. James:

> He willed to give us birth by the word of truth that we may be a kind of firstfruits of his creatures. Know this, my dear brothers: everyone should be quick to hear, slow to speak, slow to wrath. . . . Therefore, put away all filth and evil excess and humbly welcome the word that has been planted in you and is able to save your souls.
>
> Be doers of the word and not hearers only, deluding yourselves. For if anyone is a hearer of the word and not a doer, he is like a man who looks at his own face in a mirror. He sees himself, then goes off and promptly forgets what he looked like. But the one who peers into the perfect law of freedom and

65

perseveres, and is not a hearer who forgets but a doer who acts, such a one shall be blessed in what he does (Jas 1:18-25).

Before beginning our meditation on this fine passage, allow me for one moment to consider it in itself and in relation to other analogous passages in the New Testament, so that we may find it easier to grasp its own true density from the contrast, and that in the chord struck it may emit all its resonance. In a word, let us do a little exegesis.

The most obvious parallel is 1 Peter 1:23-2:2. Here we read that Christians "have been born anew, not from perishable but from imperishable seed, through the living and abiding word of God." Both texts, therefore, set out from the basic and mysterious fact of baptism and on it base the whole of the subsequent discourse. From comparison with John 1:13, we see that this re-birth does not derive from one word of God among many, but from the Word that was in the beginning with God and became flesh.

At verse 21, St. James exhorts his readers to lay aside all impurity, so as humbly to welcome the word already planted in them; St. Peter says, in almost the same words: "Rid yourselves of all malice and all deceit, insincerity . . . like newborn infants, long for pure spiritual milk." From comparison of the two texts it becomes clear that the "pure milk" is the milk of the Word. Therefore we are not talking here about purification in preparation for baptism but in preparation for hearing the Word of God, that is to say for a *further* contact with the Word. We could take James's "welcome the word" as an invitation to let the Word already received sink in deeper, hence to interiorize the Word.

At verse 22, St. James says, "Be doers of the Word and not hearers only"; the same thought is expressed by St. Paul: "It is not those who hear the law who are just in the sight of God; rather, those who observe the law will be justified" (Rom 2:13). But principally we recall the saying of Jesus that compares those who listen to the Word but do not put it into practice to people who build their house on sand, and those who do put what they have heard into practice to people who build on rock (cf. Matt 7:24f.). (Note the affinity between Jesus' imagery of building on sand and James's imagery of glancing into a mirror. In both the insubstantial nature of the thing is stressed; taking a hasty look at oneself

66

in a mirror is like writing in or building on sand and painting on air.)

Finally, at verse 25 St. James recommends his readers to fix their gaze on the Word, to linger over it, in order to become "doers who act," for blessed only are they who put the Word into effect. This reminds us of Jesus' words: "If you understand this, blessed are you if you do it" (John 13:17); "Rather, blessed are those who hear the Word of God and observe it" (Luke 11:28). Blessedness is only for those who "do" the Word.

1. An itinerary of Christian life, based on the Word

From these texts we can extract an itinerary of Christian life, complete in itself. This itinerary consists of three fundamental moments or elements.

First, the moment of *welcoming, or listening to, the Word.* This embraces all the forms and means by which we come into contact with the Word of God: from the most solemn, which is the proclamation of the Word in the liturgy (in which we receive the "pure milk" of the Word directly from the breast of Mother Church), to the humblest, which is our private Bible reading, or listening to a sermon.

Second, the moment of *reflecting on, or contemplating, the Word* (the "fixing of our gaze," of lingering over the Word). In this we assimilate the Word of God, we interiorize it, we enter into living, personal contact with it, we allow it to permeate us through and through, to illuminate our entire interior universe with its light: our thoughts, affections, and desires.

Third, the moment of *putting the Word into practice,* what Scripture calls "doing" the Word, putting it into effect by interior decisions or concrete exterior deeds, depending on what from time to time it may command us to do.

Since the entire will and perfection of God is enshrined in Scripture, this route is such as can lead the soul to the highest degree of holiness, to full and total conformity with the divine will. This spiritual itinerary, made up of listening to the Word, contemplating it, and putting it into effect, immediately brings to mind what occurs in the Eucharist. There, too, we go from welcoming Christ in the mysteries, to the contemplation or remembering of the mystery received, and then to imitating it in life. Once again we discover the profound unity of Word and Eucharist, two different sides of the same mystery.

The characteristic these two spiritual itineraries have in common is that both set out from the work of God, the mystery that comes to meet us and freely anticipates us, in the one case through Christ's Body and in the other through Christ's Word. St. James's discourse on the Word sets out, as we have seen, from baptism. So God's grace, the gift, comes first of all—not ascetic effort on our part. The work of our salvation rests on the sure foundation of God's gratuitous love. This is important because it safeguards the unique and unmistakable character of the Christian revelation: "We love because he first loved us" (1 John 4:19). We can approach God because he has approached us first.

Another fundamental characteristic common to both these paths to holiness is that in them an antithesis or mutual exclusion between the contemplative and active life has no meaning, since they embrace both. Contemplation appears as the connecting link and necessary condition for passing from communion with Christ to imitation of Christ, from hearing the Word to obeying the Word.

This basic vision of Christian life shows how much agreement there is between East and West in the spiritual sphere. Just as the route based on the mysteries has been familiar to Orthodoxy, so that based on the Word has been familiar to Latin spirituality, up to the *devotio moderna*. Medieval Western spirituality, as direct heir to the Fathers of the Church, was nourished on the Word of God, on *lectio divina*. Even contemplation and the most exalted mysticism—such as that of St. Bernard or St. Bonaventure—was not other than a form of scriptural interpretation; it fed on the Word of God and expressed itself with the Word of God. The mystical was one of the four senses, and the highest one, of Scripture.

These medieval masters have left us splendid syntheses of their spiritual interpretation of the Bible. The best known is by the Carthusian Guigo II called *A Letter on the Contemplative Life,* or *The Ladder for Monks.* What they propose, as can already be seen from this last title, is conditioned by a period when spirituality was bound up with the monastic life. However for my part I should like to show, starting from the passage in St. James, how the spiritual itinerary based on the Word of God is accessible to all and destined for all (as was the apostle's intention when he wrote those words) and to show, above all, how it does not come to a halt with contemplation, but impels to action.

2. Listening to the Word

The first stage on this road, as we have seen, is listening to the Word: "Be each of you ready to listen . . . Welcome the Word humbly . . ." This embraces all the forms and modes by which the Christian nowadays comes into contact with the Word of God: listening to the Word in the liturgy, already made easier by the use of the vernacular and by the wise choice of the texts distributed throughout the year; then Bible study groups, written aids, and—irreplaceable—private Bible reading at home. For anyone called to teach others there is, moreover, systematic Bible study: exegesis, biblical theology, and study of the original languages. "The sacred Synod," we read in *Dei Verbum,* "forcefully and specifically exhorts all the Christian faithful, especially those who live the religious life, to learn 'the surpassing knowledge of Jesus Christ' (Phil 3:8) by frequent reading of the divine Scriptures. . . . Let them go gladly to the sacred text, whether in the sacred liturgy, or in devout reading, or to suitable exercises and other approved helps."[1]

All this is indispensable and desired by the Church. There is, however, one danger against which we must be on our guard: that of stopping at this stage and transforming the personal reading of the Word of God into an impersonal reading. This is a very great danger today, particularly in the academic environment of seminaries and university faculties, that is, precisely where a proper use of the Bible should be taught. This would not be "looking at oneself *in* the mirror" as St. James recommended, but confining oneself to looking *at* the mirror! Kierkegaard observes that if one were to wait, before allowing oneself to be personally summoned by the Word, until one has solved all the problems connected with the scriptural text, the variants, and the divergences of opinion among the scholars, one would never be done. Indeed, such dallying becomes a ruse to defend oneself against the Word of God. The Word of God has been given to be put into practice and not that one may exercise oneself in exegesis of its obscurities. There is such a thing as "hermeneutic inflation" and, what is worse, people come to believe that the most important thing about the Bible is hermeneutics and not practice. "Oh, depth of cunning! They make God's word something impersonal, objective, a doctrine—whereas instead it is as God's voice that you should hear it."[2]

3. Contemplating the Word

Reading and study of the Word of God are therefore important, from a spiritual point of view, only if they are done in view of something else, not if they are ends in themselves. Even when it is pushed to the highest degree of specialization, the critical reading of the Bible in fact only constitutes the first step of the ladder. At the outset of *The Ladder of Monks,* Guigo II relates the experience from which the book took shape:

> One day, when I was busy working with my hands, I began to think about our spiritual work, and all at once four stages in spiritual exercise came into my mind: reading, meditation, prayer, and contemplation. These make a ladder for monks by which they are lifted up from earth to heaven. . . . *Reading* is the careful study of the Scriptures, concentrating all one's powers on it. *Meditation* is the busy application of the mind to seek with the help of one's own reason for knowledge of hidden truth. *Prayer* is the heart's devoted turning to God to drive away evil and obtain what is good. *Contemplation* is when the mind is in some sort lifted up to God and held above itself, so that it tastes the joys of everlasting sweetness. . . . Reading seeks for the sweetness of a blessed life, meditation perceives it, prayer asks for it, contemplation tastes it. Reading, as it were, puts food whole into the mouth, meditation chews it and breaks it up, prayer extracts its flavor, contemplation is the sweetness itself which gladdens and refreshes. . . . Reading without meditation is sterile, meditation without reading is liable to error, prayer without meditation is lukewarm, meditation without prayer is unfruitful; prayer when it is fervent wins contemplation, but to obtain it without prayer would be rare, even miraculous.[3]

We must now move on to the second phase of our itinerary, to the attitude of personal involvement and reaction to the Word. We need to look at ourselves in the mirror, without waiting to finish illuminating every detail of the mirror itself (something that can never be achieved). Let us now talk about contemplating the Word, not in the highest sense of infused contemplation (in which the author I have just quoted meant it) but in the more general sense, accessible to everyone of reflection, of dialogue with the Word, of calm and protracted gazing at the Word: to enter the presence of the Word and be "alone with the Word."

We are talking about an operation of grace, a mysterious fact, of which there is not, I can safely say, a single even slightly committed Christian who has not some time or another experienced. It is like passing through the veil of the letter to enter God's sanctuary. We can compare it to the moment described in Psalm 84: the soul that yearns and pines for the courts of the Lord has inwardly resolved to make the sacred journey, to go on pilgrimage to Jerusalem; it feels its fervor growing stronger as it goes until, having passed through "the vale of weeping" (the laborious study of the letter), it appears before God in Zion and can unburden its heart in prayer: "Lord God of hosts, hear my prayer. . . . I had rather spend one day in your courts than a thousand elsewhere."

The soul that gazes at itself in the mirror of the Word comes to know "how it is," learns to know itself, discovers how unlike the image of God and the image of Christ it is. "I do not seek my own glory," Jesus says (John 8:50): lo, the mirror is before us and at once we can see how far we are from Jesus. "Blessed are the poor in spirit": again the mirror is before us and instantly we discover that we are still full of attachments and superfluities. "Love is patient . . .": behold, before the pure mirror of charity which the Apostle holds up to our eyes, we realize how impatient, envious, selfish we are. But the mirror is a compassionate one; it only displays our deformity so as to cure it.

In this mirror of the Word we do not merely see ourselves; more importantly, we see God's face, or, better, we see God's heart. Scripture, says St. Gregory the Great, "is a letter from God Almighty to his creature; in it we come to know God's heart through God's words."[4] So Jesus' saying is true of God as well: "From the fullness of the heart the mouth speaks" (Matt 12:34). God has spoken to us, in Scripture, about what fills his heart, and what fills his heart is love. All the Scriptures were written for this purpose: that human beings might grasp how much God loves them and grasp it so as to become inflamed with love for him.[5]

St. Paul, while speaking about love, says that in this life we see God "as in a mirror" (1 Cor 13:12). This mirror is first and foremost Scripture. What can be known about God by the intellect—his invisible perfections—can be contemplated in what he has made (cf. Rom 1:20), in creation; but that which cannot be known about God by the mere intellect—his depths and secrets—can only be contemplated in Scripture. By means of the Word of God there comes about the most sublime and mysterious event possible: the living contact of our intellect with God's truth as it reveals itself to us.

In this way contemplation of the Word procures the two most important types of knowledge for us to advance along the path of true wisdom: knowledge of the self and knowledge of God. Knowledge of God without knowledge of self leads to presumption; knowledge of self without knowledge of God leads to despair. "May I know myself and may I know you," St. Augustine says to God, "may I know myself so as to become humble and may I know you so as to love you."[6] St. Francis used to spend his nights repeating: "Who are you, Lord, and who am I?"[7] The Word of God is the only one that can answer these questions.

For discovering ourselves and God in the Word, we have within ourselves a valuable help, an exegete ever to hand; I mean our soul. There is a certain affinity between our soul and Scripture: both bear within themselves the image of God and the one can therefore help us to understand the other. The mirror which is our soul differs, however, from the mirror of Scripture: it is not so pure; it is made dim by sin; it is like a well full of earth and rubbish. That is why St. James and St. Peter exhort us "to put away all impurity and malice" when we approach the Word of God; and therefore a continual purifying of the heart is needed for us to welcome the Word. Commenting on the text in Proverbs which says, "Drink water from your own cistern, running water from your own well" (Prov 5:15), Origen writes:

> You too must attempt to have your own well and your own
> spring, so that you too, when you take up a book of the Scrip-

tures, may begin even from your own understanding to bring
forth some meaning, and in accordance with those things which
you have learnt in church, you too must attempt to drink from
the fountain of your own abilities. You have a kind of "living
water" within you. Within you there are perennial veins and
streams flowing with rational understanding, as long as they
have not been filled up with earth and rubbish. But get busy
to dig out your earth and to clean out the filth, that is, to
remove the idleness of your natural ability and cast out the
inactivity of your heart.[8]

Starting from what the Church has taught (i.e., from the authentic interpretation of the Word made by the magisterium and
Tradition), the ordinary Christian can discover for himself or herself new meanings and nuances in the Word of God. Experience
shows that often an ordinary soul at prayer may gather truths
and connections in the Word of God that have escaped the most
expert commentators, crammed with technical information about
the Scriptures. There is no need for us to resign ourselves to a
mere and exclusive dependence on other people's explanations or
to read what other people have written; we need to search within
ourselves, humbly, trustingly. We have a well-loved model for
this contemplation of the Word: Mary. She "kept all these things
[lit., these words], reflecting on them in her heart" (Luke 2:19);
in her own heart, Mary sought to understand the words, comparing them with each other.

4. *Doing the Word*

The text of St. James from which we set out for this meditation has one definite feature: that of urging us ever forward, of
pointing to a target, and then inviting us to go beyond it. He
warmly recommends that we listen ("Everyone should be quick
to hear"), but then he immediately adds: "If anyone is only a
hearer . . . who does not linger before the mirror . . . who does
not fix his gaze on the Word . . ." Which is as good as saying
that listening, reading, study, exegesis are not in themselves
enough, that there has to be individual contemplation, too. But
he does not leave us alone even at contemplation, for he goes on
to say, "Be among those who put the Word into practice."

73

Here we are then, propelled into the third phase of our spiritual journey, which is plainly nearer St. James's heart and the heart of Jesus too, who said, "My mother and my brothers are those who hear the Word of God and act on it" (Luke 8:21). Without this "acting on the Word," everything remains illusion, building on sand. Besides, acting on the Word is also the best way to come to understand the Word. St. Gregory the Great makes compassion his example: someone reads Christ's words, "Give alms . . ." (Luke 11:41), takes them to heart, and starts practicing them. "Having now begun being compassionate by almsgiving, he reads other divinely authoritative words and *from experience* later grasps everything said about compassion. He reads: 'I was a father to the needy' [Job 29:16], a sentence that in reading he may previously have overlooked but which, now that compassion has started to take root in his heart, he reads, understanding what to be a father to the needy means, and so, looking into himself, he understands within what he has heard without."[9] In this way contemplation prepares for execution, and execution deepens comprehension.

But there is one important observation to be made: we need to start at once, not put delays between comprehension and execution. We human beings are all, to lesser or greater degree, absent-minded observers; we quickly forget. Things seen in the mirror, even those that make a great impression, fade away if we do not at once try to do something of what we have seen. We must resolutely say: How can I start putting this word God has given me into practice *now?* It seems incredible but this question rarely wants for an immediate reply; in one way or another we can always make a start on doing something, if only by acknowledging how far away we are, by repenting, by fixing the exact time and place at which we will do whatever it is the Word of God has shown us. Suppose, Kierkegaard acutely observes, that to someone the mirror of the Word has revealed a bad habit (he gives as his example a passion for gambling, but we can substitute our own besetting weakness). If he says to himself, "I solemnly vow by all that is holy that I shall nevermore have anything to do with gambling; tonight shall be the last time!" that man is lost. Instead, what he ought to say to himself is: "Very well, you will be allowed to gamble for the rest of your life, every blessed day, but tonight you must let it alone!" If he keeps this resolution, he is saved; he will not gamble anymore. "The first man's resolution was a knavish trick played by lust, but the second man's is a way of hoaxing lust."[10]

In this way, the Word of God indeed becomes, as Jesus said, the instrument that "prunes" our lives, that cuts away the dry and useless branches, so that we are cleaned by the Word and can bear "ever more fruit" (John 15:2-3).

Nowadays we are having a big problem with spiritual direction, because there seem in fact to be hardly any spiritual directors. It is of course good news that the problem is making itself felt, for this is a sign that there are souls who have set out on the gospel road and are looking for a guide. In such a situation, we should make clear that the Word of God assures any soul that needs it of fundamental and, in itself, infallible spiritual direction. There is, so to speak, an extraordinary spiritual direction which imposes itself at special moments when serious decisions and choices have to be made. Often in such cases God reveals his will through a word in the Bible, either heard at home or purposely sought, as happened to Anthony the Abbot, Francis of Assisi, and many other saints. So, too, today, many Christians experience these decisive words of God, which have in them the power to change the course of our lives.

Such words, received in particular moments and circumstances, are to be jealously treasured in the heart and, if possible, on paper or by some other external sign, since they are like milestones to which we ought often subsequently to refer. The prophet Jeremiah exhorted the Jews who were going into exile in Babylon "to set up road markers, put up guideposts" (Jer 31:21) along the way, so that one day they could more easily find the way home. Possibly inspired by this text, an ancient author wrote: "A traveller who has set out on a long, hard, rugged journey and fears he may lose the way home, will set signs and markers along his route, making it easy to find his way home; and the man who makes progress in sobriety will set words like standing-stones, he too fearing the same thing."[11] Seen like this, the spiritual life is as it were a road marked out by words of God.

But there is also, we may say, an ordinary and daily spiritual direction which consists in discovering God's will in the various situations in which we commonly find ourselves in life, be they human or spiritual. One such direction is assured by meditation on the Word of God accompanied by the inward unction of the Spirit, who translates the Word into good inspiration, and the good inspiration into a practical solution. The Word of God assures the two things essential to all spiritual direction: knowledge of God's will and the discerning of spirits. The Epistle to the Hebrews says of the Word of God that it can "discern reflections and thoughts of the heart" (Heb 4:12), that it effects the discerning of spirits and intentions. It is no ordinary mirror, limited to reflecting the surface of things; it is a penetrating mirror, searching within. A human being may be deceived, but not the Word of God; if one simply lets it work and does not hide things deliberately, it will infallibly reveal the real motive for what one says or does: whether it is God's glory or one's own. In this respect it is indeed a two-edged sword, sharply separating the things of God from human constraints.

There have been souls who have become saints with this sole spiritual director, the Word of God. "In the gospel," wrote St. Thérèse of Lisieux, "I find everything needful for my poor soul. In it I constantly discover new lights, hidden and mysterious meanings. I understand and know from experience that 'the kingdom of God is within us' [cf. Luke 17:21]. Jesus has no need of books or doctors to teach souls; he, the Doctor of doctors, teaches without the sound of words."[12]

Let us end this meditation by adopting as our own the very beautiful prayer St. Augustine raises to God in his *Confessions,* to obtain understanding of the Word of God:

> Let your Scriptures be my chaste delight. Let me neither be deceived in them nor deceive others by them. . . . Listen to my soul and hear its cry from the depths. . . . Grant me a space for my meditations on the hidden things of your law, and do not close your law against me when I knock. For it was not for nothing that you willed that so many pages should be filled with the writing of such dark secrets. . . . O Lord, perfect me and reveal those pages to me! See, your voice is my joy; your voice surpasses all abundance of pleasures. Give me what I love. . . . Do not forsake your grass that is thirsty for you. . . . May the inner secrets of your words be laid open to me when I knock. This I beg by our Lord Jesus Christ. . . . in whom are hidden all the treasures of wisdom and knowledge [Col 2:3]. These are the treasures I seek in your books.[13]

NOTES

1. *Dei Verbum* 25.
2. Søren Kierkegaard, *For Self-examination* (OUP, 1946) 64.
3. Guigo II, *The Ladder of Monks* (Oxford, 1978) 81–95.
4. St. Gregory the Great, *Registri Epistolarum* 4.31 (PL 77, 706).
5. St. Augustine, *De catechizandis rudibus* 1.8 (PL 40, 319).
6. St. Augustine, *Soliloquies* 2.1 (PL 32, 885).
7. *Considerations on the Holy Stigmata* 3 (St. Francis of Assisi, *Writings . . .*, p. 1446).
8. Origen, *In Genesim homilia* 12.5 (PG 12, 229).
9. St. Gregory the Great, *In Ezechielem* 1.10.31 (CCL 142, p. 159).
10. Kierkegaard, *For Self-examination,* 69.
11. Esicho Sinaita, *De temperantia et virtute* 131 (PG 93, 1521).
12. St. Thérèse of Lisieux, *Manuscript A,* 236.
13. St. Augustine, *Confessions* 11.2.2-4.

Chapter VIII

"THE LETTER BRINGS DEATH BUT THE SPIRIT GIVES LIFE"

The spiritual interpretation of the Bible

I should like to begin this meditation by adopting St. Francis of Assisi's opening words in his *Letter to all the Faithful:* "I am the servant of all and so I am bound to wait upon everyone and make known to them the fragrant words of my Lord"[1] He calls Christ's words "fragrant," thereby implicitly comparing them to sweet-smelling, newly baked bread, and we shall see in this meditation that this is exactly what God's words are: fragrant with the Holy Spirit.

1. *Scripture divinely inspired*

In the Second Epistle to Timothy we find the famous statement: "All Scripture is inspired by God" (2 Tim 3:16). The expression translated as "inspired by God" in the original Greek is one single word, *theopneustos,* which combines two words, "God" (*theos*) and "Spirit" (*pneuma*). This word has two basic meanings, one well known and another habitually neglected yet no less important than the first.

Let us begin with the well-known meaning. This is the passive meaning, emphasized in all modern translations: Scripture is "inspired by God." Another passage in the New Testament explains what this means: "Human beings [i.e., the prophets], moved by the holy Spirit spoke under the influence of God" (2 Pet 1:21). This is, in a word, the classic doctrine of the divine inspiration of Scripture, which we proclaim in the Creed as an article of faith

78

when we say that the Holy Spirit is he "who has spoken through the prophets."

This doctrine carries us back to the very source of the whole Christian mystery, which is the Trinity, the unity of and distinction between the three divine Persons. The Holy Spirit accompanies the Word just as, in the bosom of the Trinity, the breathing of the Holy Spirit is bound up with the begetting of the Word. As, at the incarnation, the Spirit enters Mary so that the Word will become flesh within her, so, in an analogous though not identical way, the Spirit works within the sacred writer, so that he can welcome the Word of God and "incarnate" it in human language. This in itself mysterious event of inspiration we can represent for ourselves in human imagery: with his divine finger (i.e., his living energy), which is the Holy Spirit, God touches that hidden point where the human spirit opens to the infinite, and from there that touch (in itself very simple and instantaneous, as is God who produces it) is diffused like a sonorous vibration through all the human faculties (will, intelligence, imagination, emotion), translating itself into concepts, images, and words. Human beings "moved by the Holy Spirit spoke under the influence of God": the mysterious transition occurs from divine motion to created reality, which can be observed in all the *ad extra* works of God: in creation, in the incarnation, in the production of grace.

The result thus obtained is a theandric reality, fully divine and fully human, the two intimately fused together, though not "confused." The magisterium of the Church (the encyclical letters *Providentissimus Deus* of Leo XIII and *Divino afflante Spiritu* of Pius XII) tells us that the two realities—divine and human—are maintained intact. God is the principal author of Scripture since he is responsible for what is written, determining its content by the activity of his Spirit. Nevertheless, the sacred writer is also the author in the full sense of the word, since he has intrinsically collaborated in this act by means of a normal human activity which God has used as an instrument. God, the Fathers used to say, is like a musician who by touching the strings of the lyre makes them vibrate; the sound is entirely the work of the musician but it would not exist were it not for the lyre-strings. In the case of Scripture, the mystery consists in the fact that God moves not inert, inanimate strings, but free ones (the will, the intelligence) which are capable of moving themselves. Only he can move such strings as he pleases while still maintaining their freedom intact and therefore acting through them.

Of this marvellous work of God, only one effect is usually emphasized: the inerrancy of Scripture, that is to say the fact that the Bible contains no error (if by "error" we mean the absence of a truth humanly possible in a given cultural context and hence one to be demanded of the writer). But biblical inspiration is the basis for much more than the mere (negative) inerrancy of the Word of God; positively, it is the basis for its inexhaustibility, its divine force and vitality, and what St. Augustine called its *mira profunditas,* its marvellous depth.

So now we are ready to investigate that other, lesser-known meaning of biblical inspiration. In itself, grammatically speaking, the participle *theopneustos* is active, not passive, and if it is true that tradition and theology have alike always explained it in a passive sense ("inspired by God"), it is also true that the same tradition has found an active significance in it too. Scripture, said St. Ambrose, is *theopneustos* not only because it is "inspired by God" but also because it "respires God," because it breathes God.[2] It is, St. Francis would say, the fragrance of God. Speaking of the creation, St. Augustine says that God did not make things and then turn his back on them, but that they "are from him and also in him."[3] The same is true of God's words: having come from God, they remain in him and he in them. Having dictated Scripture, the Holy Spirit is, as it were, contained in it, lives in it, and enlivens it unceasingly with his own divine breath. The conciliar constitution *Dei Verbum* also picks up this thread of tradition; it says that "the sacred Scriptures, inspired by God [passive inspiration!] and committed to writing once and for all time, present God's own Word in an unalterable form, and they make the voice of the Holy Spirit sound again and again in the words of the prophets and apostles" [active inspiration!]."[4]

Once again we ought to recognize the wonderful relationship between the mystery of the Eucharist and that of the Word of God. In the Mass—through the epiclesis and consecration—the Holy Spirit gives us the Eucharist, and then, in Communion, the Eucharist gives us the Holy Spirit. Once and for all time, the Holy Spirit inspired Scripture and now, each time we open the book, Scripture breathes the Holy Spirit! There are inspirations that move our will to the good, illuminations that clear our mind, our deepest emotions. . . . To what can we compare the word of Scripture? St. Gregory the Great wondered, and then replied: It is like a flint, cold to the touch, but when struck by the steel it gives off sparks and lights the fire. The words of Scripture stay cold if one limits them to their literal meaning, but if, inspired by the Lord, one strikes with an attentive mind, they will give vent to the fire of mystic meanings.[5]

I once heard a man give this testimony in public: He had reached the last stage of alcoholism; he couldn't hold out for more than an hour or two without a drink; wherever he happened to be, travelling, in the train, or at work, his first thought was where could he get some wine. His wife, who was there too, said she had reached the brink of despair and could see no way out for herself and her three children, except death. Someone invited them to some Bible readings. There was one word in particular which, heard by chance, made a deep impression on him and which for many years served as a rope to draw him up from the abyss. Each time he read it over, it was like a fresh flood of heat and strength, until he was completely cured. When he tried to tell us what that word was, his voice broke and he was so overcome with emotion that he could not manage to complete the sentence. It was the verse in the Song of Songs (1:2) which says, "More delightful is your love than wine." It would have been easy for any "expert" on the Song to show him that the verse had no bearing on his situation and that he was deluding himself, but the man went on repeating, "I was dead and now I am alive. That word gave me back my life!" So, too, the man born blind replied to those who questioned him, "How that may be, I don't know. All I do know is, before I couldn't see and now I can see" (cf. John 9:25).

2. "The letter brings death": biblical Ebionism

But now we must confront the most delicate of problems: How are we to approach the Scriptures so as to release the Spirit that they contain? How are we to explain the Scriptures, that is, taking the term literally, how are we to smooth out their folds so that they may indeed exhale the divine fragrance which, by faith, we know is stored within them? I have already said that Scripture is a theandric (i.e., divine-human) reality. Now, the law of any theandric reality (e.g., Christ and the Church) is that the divine element cannot be discovered in it except as it is approached by way of the human. One cannot discover the divinity in Christ except through his concrete humanity. Those who, in antiquity, claimed to do otherwise fell into *Docetism;* despising Christ's body and human characteristics as mere "appearances" (*dokein*), they also mislaid his profound reality, and instead of a living God made man, they were left with merely their own idea of God. Similarly, one cannot discover the Spirit in Scripture except through the letter, that is, by way of the concrete human dress that the Word of God has assumed in the various books and inspired authors. One cannot discover the divine meaning in them except by setting out from the human meaning, the intention of the human author: Isaiah, Jeremiah, Luke, Paul, and so forth.

In this process, the immense effort of study and research in connection with the Scriptures finds its full justification. There are hosts of believers who spend their lives in elucidating biblical problems: problems concerning the very text of Scripture, the historical and cultural context of each book, the internal and external sources of the Bible, the exact meaning of each passage, etc. Christians owe these scholars a great debt of gratitude; opening our Bible, without even being aware of their labor, we gather its fruits by the handful and are enriched.

But our enthusiasm is soon veiled in sadness. Again taking the example of the person of Jesus, there was not only the danger of Docetism, neglecting the human; there was also the danger of stopping short at the latter and not seeing anything in him but the human, not discovering the divine dimension of Son of God. There was, in a word, the danger of *Ebionism.*

For the Ebionites (who were Jewish Christians), Jesus was indeed a great prophet, perhaps the greatest of the prophets, but nothing more. They did not make the qualitative leap: they were stuck in the Old Testament although they were living in the New, since they had not grasped the true newness. The Fathers called them "Ebionites" (from *ebionim,* poor men), meaning that they were poor in faith.

This happens with regard to Scripture too; the risk exists of halting at the letter, of considering the Bible an excellent book, perhaps the most excellent of human books, but a solely human one. In the one case as in the other (i.e., in the case of Docetism as of Ebionism), we are dealing with heresy in the most classic sense of the term, that is, partial choice, breach of unity, impoverishment, and therefore, since God is concerned, sin. The sin of dividing Scripture exists, just as for Paul the sin of dividing Christ exists (cf. 1 Cor 1:13).

Unfortunately we are now experiencing the danger of reducing Scripture to a single dimension. The breach of unity today is based not on Docetism but on Ebionism. We are "poor people," but with an unhappy poverty, not a blessed one, for there is no worse poverty than to do without God. Kierkegaard wrote some words which at the distance of a century still keep a good part of their validity: "How is God's word read in Christendom? If we were to distinguish two classes (for we cannot here concern ourselves with individual exceptions), one might say that the greater part never read God's word, and that a smaller part read it learnedly in one fashion or another, that is to say, do not really read God's word, but admire the mirror. Or, to say the same thing in another way, the greater part regard God's word as an antiquated document which one puts aside, and a smaller part regards God's word as an exceedingly notable document of olden time upon which one expends an astonishing amount of diligence and acumen."[6] To "admire the mirror" means to confine ourselves to critical problems, to the letter of Scripture.

Many scholars expounding the Bible deliberately confine themselves to the historico-critical method, and this not only outside the Church, within the various critical and liberal schools (which has been going on since the eighteenth century), but inside the Church as well, among many exegetes who profess to be believers and Catholics. The secularization of the sacred has nowhere revealed itself so acutely as in the secularization of the sacred Scriptures. Yet, to claim to understand Scripture exhaustively by studying it exclusively with the instrument of historico-philological analysis, is like claiming to discover what the Eucharist is through a chemical analysis of the consecrated host. Historico-critical analysis, even when carried to the heights of perfection, only represents the first step in knowledge of the Bible, the step concerning the letter.

Jesus solemnly affirms that Abraham "saw his day" (cf. John 8:56), that Moses had "written about him" (cf. John 5:46), that

Isaiah "saw his glory and spoke about him" (cf. John 12:41), that the prophets and psalms and all the Scriptures speak of him (cf. Luke 24:27, 44; John 5:39). The Fathers were convinced that "the Son of God is implanted everywhere throughout the Scriptures."[7] But nowadays so-called scientific exegesis hesitates to speak of Christ, no longer discerns him in virtually any passage of the Old Testament or, at least, is nervous of saying that he can be discerned there, for fear of being written off as "unscientific."

The most serious drawback of a certain kind of excessively scientific and "objective" exegesis is that it completely alters the relationship between the exegete and the Word of God. The Bible becomes an object which the professor has "mastered" and before which (like any scientist) he or she is neutral, whereas in this unique case it is neither permissible to stay neutral, nor is it given to anyone to master the subject, since we have to let it master us. To say that a believer-scholar has mastered the Word of God, is, properly speaking, to utter a blasphemy. To act thus with the Word of God is "as if a rod could sway him who lifts it, or a staff him who is not wood" (Isa 10:15).

The consequence of all this is the closing up and folding in of Scripture on itself. It goes back to being the "sealed" book, the "veiled" book, for—says St. Paul—the veil is taken away through Christ whenever a person "turns to the Lord," recognizes Christ in the pages of Scripture (cf. 2 Cor 3:15-16). What happens with certain very sensitive plants that fold their leaves as soon as they are touched by a foreign body, or with certain shells that close their valves to preserve the pearl they have inside, also happens with the Bible. The pearl of Scripture is Christ. In short, we witness a sort of self-defence on the part of the Word of God; it rejects the foreign body that ventures on to its ground out of mere curiosity. It is like (I am only making a comparison!) the angel of the Lord repulsing Heliodorus, flinging him to the ground, scourging him, and enveloping him in "great darkness" when he entered the Temple of Jerusalem to steal its treasures (2 Macc 3:24f.).

It is hard otherwise to explain all the crises of faith among biblical scholars, some of whom have even ended by leaving the sacred ministry. Talking to one of them, I was amazed at his inability to perceive any truly divine and supernatural dimension in Scripture. When we wonder why spiritual poverty and aridity dominate some of our seminaries and training establishments, it does not take long to realize that one of the main reasons is the way Scripture is being taught in them. The Church has lived and lives by the spiritual interpretation of the Bible; cut off this canal which nourishes the devout life, zeal, and faith, and everything dries up and withers. Even the liturgy loses its meaning or comes to be experienced as something quite divorced from one's own cultural life, since the liturgy is entirely constructed on a spiritual interpretation of Scripture.

Having seen these things for myself, I now understand why St. Paul wrote that, of itself, "the letter brings death" (2 Cor 3:6), and I also understand those terrible words bequeathed by our Father, St. Francis, to us Friars Minor in one of his admonitions: "They are slain by the letter who only crave to know the words of it, so that they can pass as more learned than others and acquire great riches to leave to their relatives and friends. And those religious are slain by the letter who have no will to follow the spirit of God's written word, but rather desire to know only the text and explain it to others."[8]

3. *"The Spirit gives life"*

When we don't use a limb for a long while, it needs to undergo rehabilitation exercises before it can be used properly again. For all too long, Christians have been without the use of this vital "limb," the Bible, and now they need to be retrained in how to use it. For some people, retraining will consist at first in picking up the Bible and reading it, since perhaps they have never seriously approached it before, or not at full length. For others who know the Bible and have even perhaps studied it for some time, retraining will consist in reaccustoming oneself to that spiritual interpretation of Scripture which throughout the patristic and medieval periods constituted the main source of the Church's wisdom and spirituality.

A very hopeful sign is that several eminent exegetes are already becoming aware of this need. One recently wrote: "It is a matter of urgency that anyone studying and interpreting Scripture should give serious thought to the exegesis of the Fathers, so as behind their methods to rediscover the spirit that inspired them, the depth of soul that inspired their exegesis; we should learn to interpret Scripture at their school, not merely from the historical and critical point of view, but equally within the Church and for the Church" (I. de la Potterie). Henri de Lubac, in a justly famous work on medieval exegesis, has revealed the consistency, soundness, and extraordinary fecundity of the spiritual exegesis practiced by the ancient and medieval Fathers.

But it must be said that the Fathers, in this field, only applied (with the imperfect instruments then at their disposal) the straightforward lesson of the New Testament. In other words, they were not the initiators but the bearers of a tradition which had for its founders John, Paul, and Jesus himself. These latter had always not only practiced a spiritual interpretation of the Scriptures (i.e., a reading with reference to Christ), but had even provided the justification for reading the Scriptures like this by declaring that all the Scriptures speak of Christ (cf. John 5:39), that "the Spirit of Christ" was already at work in them, expressing himself through the prophets (cf. 1 Pet 1:11) and that everything in the Old Testament is said by way of allegory, with reference to the Church (cf. Gal 4:24).

However, by "spiritual interpretation" of the Bible we do not mean an edifying, mystical, subjective or, even worse, a fanciful interpretation, as opposed to a scientific interpretation which would, by contrast, be objective. Not at all: the spiritual interpretation is the most objective there can be, since it is based on the Spirit of God and not on human wit. The subjective interpretation of Scripture (based on free examination) has run riot precisely when spiritual interpretation has been given up and most blatantly abandoned.

Spiritual interpretation is very precise and objective; it is interpretation done under the guidance, or by the light, of the Holy Spirit, who inspired the Scriptures in the first place. It is based on an historical event, that is, the redemptive act of Christ, who by his death and resurrection completes the plan of salvation, fulfills all types and prophecies, unveils all hidden mysteries, and offers us the true key for interpreting the whole Bible. Anyone choosing to read the Scriptures after Christ's life while disregarding his act would be like someone persistently reading a musical score in the key of G when the composer has already moved into the key of B; every single note after the shift would sound false and out of tune. The New Testament calls the new key "the Spirit," while it defines the old key as "the letter," saying that "the letter brings death, but the Spirit gives life" (2 Cor 3:6). Reading the Scriptures without the Holy Spirit would be like opening a book in the dark.

To erect an antithesis between "letter" and "Spirit" does not mean erecting one between Old and New Testaments, as though the former merely represented the letter and the latter only the Spirit. It means, rather, to make an antithesis between the two different ways of reading either the Old Testament or the New: between the way which disregards Christ, and the way which, by contrast, evaluates everything by the light of Christ. This is why the Church prizes both Testaments, for both speak to her of Christ. When the Word of God is read like this, a sort of transfiguration of Scripture occurs, analogous to Christ's transfiguration on Tabor. The Spirit hidden within the Scriptures sets them ablaze from within, making him known whom they were foreshadowing.

So, spiritual interpretation confers new and hitherto unknown force and influence on the Old Testament, but this only comes about once we realize that it is talking about something else; that besides having a concrete and literal meaning, it also has a symbolic one leading us beyond it. In other, more traditional, words, the text becomes powerful once we discover that it is speaking "by allegory" (Gal 4:24). St. Augustine says,

> Anything that is suggested by means of symbols strikes and kindles our affection much more forcefully than the truth itself would do if presented unadorned with mysterious symbols. . . . Our sensibility is less easily kindled when still involved in purely concrete realities, but if it is first turned towards symbols drawn from the corporeal world, and thence again to the plane of those spiritual realities signified by those symbols, it gathers strength by the mere act of passing from one to the other and, like the flame of a burning torch, is made by the motion to burn all the brighter.[9]

Something similar happens for the Christian in passing from the Old Testament to the New, from prophecy to reality. In this passing, the mind "flares up" like a moving torch. The description of the sufferings of the Servant of Yahweh in Isaiah 53 has its own way of speaking to us about the passion of Christ, which no historical narrative in the Gospels can replace. Similarly, the words in Proverbs: "Wisdom has built her house . . . she has spread her table; she has sent out her handmaidens, she calls . . . 'Come, eat of my food, and drink of the wine I have mixed' " (Prov 9:5) have an evocative power that no discourse on the Eucharist can make unnecessary.

Indirect language (be it the symbolic language of the sacraments or the prophetic language of the Scriptures) is less prone, in a sense, to being exhausted, since it says and does not say; rather than assert, it suggests, brings to mind, and hence, each time, stimulates a different motion of the heart. This is why the Old Testament (e.g., the Song of Songs) has always been so dear to the mystics. The Old Testament is not scorned in spiritual interpretation; on the contrary, it is exalted to the utmost. When St. Paul says, "The Spirit gives life," this has to be understood as meaning: gives life to the letter in the Old Testament as well.

4. *What the Spirit says to the Church*

The spiritual interpretation of Scripture is not, however, concerned only with the Old Testament; in a different way it is also concerned with the New, which also should be read in a spiritual sense. Reading the New Testament spiritually means reading it by the light of the Holy Spirit given at Pentecost to the Church in order to guide her into all truth (i.e., into a full understanding and practice of the gospel).

Jesus himself explained, in anticipation, the relationship between his Word and the Spirit whom he would send (even if we have some doubt that he used precisely those words quoted in St. John's Gospel). The Spirit, we read in St. John, "will teach and remind you" of everything Jesus has said (cf. John 14:25f.), that is, will make all this understood in all its implications. He "will not speak on his own," will not say anything new with regard to what Jesus has already said but, as Jesus himself says, "will take from what is mine and reveal it to you" (John 16:14). Jesus did not say everything openly; there were matters the full weight of which the disciples were not yet in a state to bear. The

Holy Spirit is charged with leading the disciples into the fullness of the as yet unattained truths. These are not, however, completely new things, unpublished sayings, but further, deeper meanings hidden in Christ's words which the Paraclete will bring to light. To say that the Spirit guides the Church to the discovery of all truth (cf. John 16:13) means that he guides her to the discovery of all truth hidden in the words and actions of Jesus. In fact, there is no other truth than the Truth which Jesus is! We are living in the midst of this progressive revelation by the Spirit and perhaps much more numerous are the matters of which we as yet are unable to bear the weight, than those which we have so far understood.

We can therefore say that the spiritual interpretation, in the full and comprehensive sense, is the one by which the Holy Spirit teaches us to read the Old Testament as referring to Jesus and to read the Old and New Testaments together as referring to the Church.

In this we can see how spiritual interpretation presupposes and goes beyond scientific interpretation. Scientific interpretation knows but one direction, which is that of history: in a word, it explains what comes after in the light of what has gone before; it explains the New Testament in the light of the Old, and explains the Church in the light of the New. A great deal of critical effort, as regards Scripture, consists in illustrating the teachings of the gospel in the light of Old Testament traditions, rabbinical exegesis, and so forth; it consists, to be brief, in a search for sources. (This is the principle on which Kittel and a great many other biblical aids are based.)

Spiritual interpretation fully recognizes the validity of this line of research but to it adds another, opposite one, made possible only by the Spirit, not by history; only by faith, not by science. It consists in explaining what goes before in the light of what comes after, prophecy in the light of its fulfilment, the Old Testament in the light of the New, and the New in the light of the Church's Tradition. In the prophet Isaiah we read these words of God: "Things of the past I foretold long ago/ they went forth from my mouth, I let you hear of them;/ then suddenly I took action and they came to be" (Isa 48:3). Only after God has taken action and carried out his plan can the meaning of what he has prepared and prefigured be fully grasped. Only after the whole mosaic has been mounted on the wall can one fully grasp the significance of each individual *tessera,* which on its own would mean next to nothing.

This is valid not only for the transition from the Old Testament to the New, but also for the transition from the New Testament to the Church, for only by the light of what the Spirit keeps accomplishing in the Church can we little by little discover the infinite potentialities and implications of the Word of God and the mystery of Christ. Tradition is, as it were, a great sounding-box for Scripture. What would be the good of a violin which only had strings to vibrate but not that wondrous cavity of selected, seasoned, and polished wood in which the sound, one might say, takes body? What would be the point of the Song of Songs, read merely as it is found in the biblical manuscripts, without the resonance it has acquired in the liturgy and spirituality of the Church, where it is applied now to the Church herself, now to Mary, and now to the soul in love with God?

If, as Jesus says, every tree is known by its fruits, the Word of God cannot be fully known before we have seen the fruits that it has produced. Studying Scripture in the light of Tradition is somewhat like getting to know the tree by its fruits. This is why Origen says that "the spiritual sense is what the Spirit gives to the Church."[10] This is identical with the Church's interpretation or directly with Tradition itself, if by Tradition we mean not only the solemn declarations of the magisterium (which in fact are concerned with very few biblical texts), but also the experience of doctrine and of holy lives in which the Word of God has, as it were, been incarnated anew and unfolded by action of the Holy Spirit in the course of the centuries.

Retraining to a spiritual understanding of Scripture does not in fact mean devaluing critical scholarship, for it remains true that in a theandric reality one can never attain the divine without passing anew by way of the human. What is needed is not a spiritual interpretation that would replace present-day scientific exegesis with a mechanical return to the exegesis of the Fathers, but rather a new kind of spiritual interpretation that would correspond to the immense progress achieved in the study of "the letter." An interpretation that would have the inspiration and faith of the Fathers and, at the same time, the consistency and earnestness of present-day biblical science. In the Church we need both scientific and spiritual experts, willing to listen to each other, respecting and valuing what each can offer the other. We need "saintly doctors," or saints and doctors, if we can't have the two combined.

5. The Spirit who blows from the four winds

Looking at the plain of dry bones, the prophet Ezekiel heard the question: "Can these bones come to life?" (Ezek 37:3). We might put the same question to ourselves today: Can exegesis, dried out by a long excess of philology, recover the drive and life it used to have at other periods in the history of the people of God? Henri de Lubac, having studied the long history of Christian exegesis, concluded rather mournfully that the conditions are lacking for us moderns to revive a spiritual method of interpretation like that of the Fathers; that we lack the soaring faith and the sense of fullness and unity that they had; that anyone trying to copy their boldness today would be virtually committing an act of profanation, not having the spirit from which these things proceeded.[11] He does not however completely close the door to hope but says that, "if we want to recover something of the spiritual interpretation of the Scriptures which existed in the early centuries of the Church, we must first produce a new spiritual movement."[12]

Thirty years later and fifteen years after the Second Vatican Council, it seems to me that these last words of his were prophetic. That "spiritual movement" and that "soaring faith" have started to come about, not because human beings have programmed or foreseen them (for how could that possibly be done?) but because the Spirit has begun to breathe anew, unexpectedly, from the four winds on the dry bones. Simultaneous with the reappearance of charisms, we observe the reappearance of the spiritual interpretation of the Bible, and this too is a fruit—and one of the most exquisite—of the Spirit. As I take part in Bible study groups and prayer meetings, I am often amazed to hear reflections on the Word of God quite similar to those made in their own day by Origen, St. Augustine, or St. Gregory the Great, even if in simpler language. The words about the Temple, about "the tent of David," about Jerusalem destroyed and rebuilt after the Exile are applied, very simply, very pertinently, to the Church, to Mary, to the local community, or to an individual's personal life. What is written about the personalities of the Old Testament leads to a consideration, by analogy or by antithesis, about Jesus, and what is narrated about Jesus is applied in up-to-date terms to the Church and the individual believer. I remember among others this prayer uttered by a woman after listening to the episode where Elijah is carried up into heaven and leaves Elisha a portion of his spirit; she said, "Thank you, Jesus, who ascending into heaven left us not merely part of your Spirit but all your Spirit! Thank you for not having left it to a single disciple but to all of us!" This is spiritual interpretation of the Bible, but that woman knew nothing of it. She had done what the Church's liturgy does when, on the thirteenth Sunday of Year C, we hear, one after the other, the call of Elisha by Elijah (1 Kgs 19:19f.) and the more demanding call of certain disciples by Jesus (Luke 9:51f.).

On that day and on many other occasions since, I have had to exclaim, like Jesus: "I give praise to you, Father, Lord of heaven and earth, for although you have hidden these things from the wise and learned you have revealed them to the childlike" (Matt 11:25).

NOTES

1. Francis of Assisi, *Letter to all the Faithful* (St. Francis of Assisi, *Writings* . . ., p. 93).
2. St. Ambrose, *De Spiritu Sancto* 3.112 (CSEL 79, p. 198).
3. St. Augustine, *Confessions* 4.12.18.
4. *Dei Verbum* 21.
5. St. Gregory the Great, *In Ezechielem* 2.10.1 (CCL 142, p. 379).
6. Kierkegaard, *For Self-examination,* 58.
7. St. Irenaeus, *Adversus Haereses* 4.10.1.
8. St. Francis of Assisi, *Admonitions* 7 (St. Francis of Assisi, *Writings* . . ., p. 81).
9. St. Augustine, *Epistula* 55.11.21 (CSEL 34, 1, p. 192).
10. Origen, *In Leviticum homilia* 5.5 (PG 12, 454).
11. Henri de Lubac, *Exégèse médiévale,* 2/2 (Paris, 1964) 79.
12. Henri de Lubac, *Histoire et Esprit* (Paris, 1950) (Conclusion).